Data Recovery

A Science of Trust and Ingenuity

Causes, Precautions, Tools, Strategies, Market Overview

1st English Edition 2021 based on 5th German Edition

Author: Christian Bartsch

English: 1st English Edition 2021

ISBN: 979-8-725597-47-9 Softcover
ISBN: 979-8-505274-81-1 Hardcover

German: 5th German Edition 2020 ISBN: 979-8-628712-39-9

Older German Edition released in: 2011, 2013, 2017, 2019
ISBN: 978-3-947256-00-6

Publisher:
ACATO GmbH, Theresienhöhe 28, 80339 Munich, Germany
www.acato.de

Revision-No. 5.2.1 ENG / 2021-05-16 — 19-00

Content

1   INTRODUCTION..**5**

2   CAUSES OF DATA LOSS...**8**

1.1   TECHNICAL REASONS FOR DATA LOSS................................ 9

    1.1.1   Hard drives and their technical issues.........................*11*

    1.1.2   Flash memory and their technical issues....................*14*

1.2   ORGANISATIONAL CAUSES OF DATA LOSS...........................21

    1.2.1   Insufficient precautions...*21*

    1.2.2   Silly Cost Cutting..*23*

1.3   DEVICE-SPECIFIC REASONS FOR FAILURE 27

    1.3.1   Hard Drive..*28*

    1.3.2   USB Hard Drive...*30*

    1.3.3   Network Array Storage (NAS) Drives........................*31*

    1.3.4   RAID Systems..*32*

    1.3.5   SSD Drives..*35*

    1.3.6   USB Pen Drives...*36*

    1.3.7   Memory Cards...*37*

1.4   DATA LOSS DUE TO SABOTAGE..39

    1.4.1   Ransomware..*39*

    1.4.2   Fax Attacks...*40*

3   DATA RECOVERY **41**

3.1   STRATEGIC APPROACH...41

3.2   ORGANISATIONAL PLANNING 42

    3.2.1   HR Planning *42*

    3.2.2   Technical Planning *43*

3.3   TECHNICAL POSSIBILITIES..43

    3.3.1   Drive Analysis *44*

    3.3.2   Memory Cards *45*

    3.3.3   USB Pen Drives...*46*

    3.3.4   USB Memory Cards..*49*

    3.3.5   Hard Drives..*50*

    3.3.6   SSD Drives *51*

    3.3.7   Raid Systems *52*

    3.3.8   Cell phones and Smartphones...................................*52*

    3.3.9   Additions to this book..*55*

3.4   MARKET OVERVIEW 58

    3.4.1   Misleading advertising..*59*

    3.4.2   Invented laboratory photos *61*

	3.4.3	Black sheep in the data recovery industry	62
	3.4.4	Can one trust a customer review (page)?	64
	3.4.5	Advertising with extremely low prices	65
	3.4.6	Global list of data recovery firms	66
	3.4.7	Training and Knowledge Exchange	69
4	**TECHNICAL EQUIPMENT**		**70**
	4.1	TOOLS FOR HARD DRIVE DATA RECOVERY	70
	4.1.1	Atola Bandura	70
	4.1.2	Acelabs PC3000 Portable/Express	70
	4.1.3	Acelabs Data Extractor	71
	4.1.4	Laminar flow Desktops (cleanrooms)	71
	4.1.5	SCSI / SAS Raid Controller	72
	4.2	EQUIPMENT FOR DATA RECOVERY FROM MEMORY CARDS AND USB PEN DRIVES	73
	4.2.1	PC3000 Flash	73
	4.2.2	VNR – Visual NAND Reconstructor (Rusolut)	73
	4.2.3	Soldering Tool for PCBs and memory chips	74
	4.2.4	Rework stations	74
	4.2.5	Stencils for reballing chips	75
	4.2.6	Holder for reballing	75
	4.2.7	Special smartphone reballing kits	76
	4.2.8	Solder Wick	76
	4.2.9	Solder Station	76
	4.2.10	Sucking pens and other helpful gadgets	77
	4.3	EQUIPMENT FOR SMARTPHONE DATA RECOVERY	77
	4.3.1	VNR (Rusolut)	77
	4.3.2	NuProg	79
	4.3.3	Easy JTag Devices	79
	4.3.4	LCD-Separators	80
	4.4	SOFTWARE PRODUCTS FOR DATA RECOVERY	80
	4.4.1	UFS Explorer	80
	4.4.2	JPEG Repair Kit	81
5	**DATA SECURITY IN COMPANIES**		**81**
	5.1	WRONG SECURITY APPROACHES	82
	5.1.1	How a NAS becomes a black hole for its data	82
	5.1.2	Errors in IT Consulting	82
	5.1.3	Using Cobit to increase security	83
6	**HOW TO PREVENT DATA LOSS**		**84**
	6.1	HAVING AN OVERVIEW OF YOUR INFRASTRUCTURE	84
	6.2	EVALUATION OF POTENTIAL WEAKNESSES	85

     6.2.1   Analyse the strategic zones..*85*
     6.2.2   Analyse your current state...*85*
   6.3   TO DO LIST..86
     6.3.1   Creating your action list..*86*
     6.3.2   Plan for a crisis...*86*
     6.3.3   Publication of crisis response strategies...............................*86*
     6.3.4   Handling internal conflicts..*87*
     6.3.5   Introduction of a Helpdesk System...*87*

7   **PROTECTION** **88**
   7.1   DEGREE OF IMPLEMENTATION 88
     7.1.1   How regulators affect us (SEC, NYSE)......................................*88*
   7.2   DEVICE DESTRUCTION 89

8   **FINAL THOUGHTS**...**90**

9   **AUTOR'S PROFILE**...**91**
   9.1   SPEECHES 91
   9.2   RADIO, TV AND MAGAZINE ARTICLES 92
     9.2.1   Vision for the future..*94*

10   **BIBLIOGRAPHY** **95**

1 Introduction

When you experience a malfunction of your PC, MacBook or other device, you do tend to be annoyed at this inconvenience. Even if you are a busy person, you need to pay attention to that device of yours. It is literally calling for help before it kicks the bucket. Of course, you might cry out loud not at me for expecting your company IT to fail or your much-loved smartphone to die on your lap. Unfortunately, most <u>electronic devices suffer</u> from **wear**, **mal treatment** and **potential malice**. In such situations it is vital to sit down and try to <u>get calm thoughts</u>. Going into irrational actions *often cause greater damage* than what just happened a few minutes ago to your device.

Before I go into further details, I would like to briefly explain the objective of my book. I published **my original book on data recovery** in the German language in **2011** and continued to publish <u>updated releases every 2-3 years</u>. You might ask, why I bother doing this at all? Over the many years of having been helping people with their computer problems and where necessary recovering lost data, I have come to realize that there is **a lot of fake information** and **misconceptions**. Some of the negativity brought towards the real data recovery professionals comes from <u>former experiences</u> people have had with **some rather questionable** data recovery companies.

Before starting to work in the data recovery field, I worked in the IT of **several large German enterprises** before venturing into becoming an entrepreneur. When I was 30, I suddenly needed a data recovery for my Raid Server. At that time, I had **just recently founded** a computer company. In my situation of not having access to the data of my business and other private data (I had stored there) - I **urgently needed that data** back.

In those times it was maybe 10-100 MB I just needed out of that 40GB IDE drive. When I got that *quote from the data recovery company* **I was shocked** at the **crazy price** and the **false claims**. My Hard drive was definitely not suffering of a head crash. I just had a messed Raid system due to a minor power failure. After receiving my drive back from them, I noticed **it was intentionally damaged**.

Since I had worked in the IT of several corporates after having been programming and handling hardware **since my 13th birthday** I knew quite well, that **there was malice** in what had happened to me. It took further 3 years before I actively became a DR professional myself and started taking lessons in the technical expertise needed for providing a professional service.

As I got more cases to work on, my knowledge grew and with the advice from other DR pros I got a better understanding how to get the job done properly. Over the time I made great friends in the community of real DR people and contributed with my own tools

While advising people who called my company for help, I tried to provide a service the way I was used from my time working in a corporate helpdesk. I quickly noticed that **there was so much to explain** that 1 phone call would not be enough. Hence, I started writing my first book and provided it to my clients. Eventually, people **gave me great feedback** and **motivated me to get it published** so that more people to benefit from the insights and on how to prevent losing data a 2nd time.

You **might think** that data recovery professionals **prefer to keep society uneducated** about the data storage technology people use every day. It is true that DR companies *make money by recovering* data after people lost their data.

Nevertheless, some types of irreversible data loss could have been prevented, had users been better educated in school and employers on how to properly treat their devices. This kind of knowledge isn't really taught in university courses for future IT professionals.

Let me now take you on an informative and hopefully also useful journey into the world of data recovery. I want you to avoid scams and treat your equipment with the necessary care they deserve from you.

Yours

Christian Bartsch

PS: If you would like to get advice on how to protect your organisation against data loss, don't hesitate to contact us. Our data centre experts around the globe can offer customized internal workshops for midsized and corporate enterprises.

Do you need more strategical insights before the day?

Get the IT strategy book: books.meetchrisbartsch.com

Don't worry! We ship printed copies worldwide.

Trust me: it is worthwhile the effort to mind feed now!

2 Causes of Data Loss

Data losses often occur due to human error or technical mal function.

Humans often don't take care when handling their devices. They belief that technology can't fail or expect others to make sure a backup exists. On the other hand, decision makers love cutting costs and replacing reliable equipment with inadequate cheaper replacements. Once the systems fail, they expect others to take the blame for their incompetency and mismanagement.

Let us first look into the reasons for equipment failing due to material aging or wear. At a later stage we will look into data loss that is caused by human interaction.

Photo: Parts of a USB Pen Drive with Hardware Encryption

1.1 Technical Reasons for Data Loss

When a hard drive or other component forces the system to fail, one often refers to a system failure. Usually, users are then confronted with a multitude of error messages. These messages are either ignored or misunderstood. That leads to additional damage and wrong response by the user or the technician trying to get the system working again.

Some of these errors you can identify even before the component manages to dominate a system failure. If your memory cards start getting errors windows will usually alert you while you are working or during shutdown of your system. I have seen in the past even very expensive servers failing just because of a part that cost less than a lunch. Unfortunately, server admins too **often think** these errors are a hint of a bad hard drive. Check and replace the RAM.

Let us focus on the hard drive related components. Most of the hard drive related accidents happen at **home** and in a busy **work** environment. These drives are attached by cable to a computer or power plug. They get up in a hurry and pull the USB hard drive off the desk, shelf or even half open drawer (favourite self-destruction method of students). When the drive hits the ground or even a medium soft object (*e.g., you catch it half way down with your hands*) the drive experiences a kinetic force. The small or large impact forces the **rotating heads** inside the drive to touch the rotating or waiting discs.

Even notebooks know how to fall off the desk or out of the balcony (had one case where the disks were only a bunch of glass shredding). With the introduction of SSDs in notebooks and thin notebooks this danger of being dropped is less lethal for your data unless you get a power surge and burn your SSD memory chips.

Looking at the risk servers are exposed you would be astonished how negligent IT staff can be. I once was told of a bunch of very expensive servers being transported 800 miles in the back of a delivery van with no cushioning nor ropes to keep it from juggling about in the back of that van. Of course, the drives were afterwards just a horrible mess and needed replacement.

On other occasions I had to handle a server with multiple hard drive slots that were so dirty that each drive needed to be cleaned (incl. me washing my hands after each drive as gloves were not helpful in the way the drives had been mounted). Accordingly, messy was the attitude of that (medium sized) company's management towards data security and proper maintenance. Many drives in that Raid system were physically damaged.

Similar human errors happen with USB pen drives, tablets and any type of smartphone. Not to mention water damage (or coke or other nasty stuff).

When humans are not to blame for data loss then its often either **wear and tear** due to **age** of the device (10+ years) or **intensive usage** (e.g., frequent traveller). Also, **material fatigue** can hit your drive no matter whether the hard drive is just 1 month or 21 years old.

The other reason is due to the continued rapid development of even greater storage capacity. The denser the data is stored the less space for avoiding **minor movement error** or **proximity related clashes** is available. In later sections on flash devices, I will explain the issue with density and proximity. Just keep in mind, data storage is still a young field of science compared to other sciences that exist for over 200+ years. We keep reinventing the type of storage devices but our cars still use round wheels (square wheels never took off really).

Photo: Heads of a hard drive

In the next sections i will be explaining the different types of devices and systems so that you have a better understanding of how they work. This will then make it easier for you to understand why they fail and how you can protect your company and your personal data against painful data loss.

1.1.1 Hard drives and their technical issues

Hard drives are rotating storage devices. When we do not refer to SSDs or SSD hard drives then its always a rotating disc inside the casing that has our data. SSD Drives store the data on memory chips!

Depending on the size and capacity of the hard drive you will find one or multiple disks. More modern drives are capable of storing data on both sides of a disc. Once the hard drive is powered up, the discs start rotating and thereby generate an air cushion. This is when the heads mounted on an "actuator" (a.k.a., heads arm) slide sideways into the disc area. The air cushion allows the heads to fly over the discs without touching the surface.

The space between discs and heads is very tiny. If people put their fingerprints on the discs, they create artificial mountains as your fingers natural residue leave a greasy mark that can dirty the heads and even make them crash or wiggle waggle to cause additional minor damage.

When a drive is dropped or hit then the heads touch the surface of the discs. Thereby, often heads, the arm and even motor can be damaged. That leads to a so-called head crash. Then you eventually hear scratching, knocking or the drive totally refuses to love the arm out. If you hear a scratching then you should remove power as the heads are scratching off the magnetic surface of the (glass) disc.

Since a hard drive consist of moving (e.g., heads, actuator, motor) and non-rotating electronic parts (PCB), a power surge and other impacts can damage electronic parts (chips). An electronic error occurs when the PCB has been damaged. Some of these chips are important to the motor or head instruction and communication with the mainboard of your PC.

Your hard drives firmware can be damaged too. This software and system related data is either stored on a special memory chip or on a reserved area of the discs. When people swap PCBs without making sure they are compatible or have been adjusted to the patient drive then that is where users create additional damage to their data.

Hard drive manufacturers often manufacture drives with the same "*model name*" or "*model code*" but use different chips or firmware on the PCB of the drives. That is why sourcing donor drives can take time and lead to the need for buying a donor drive that costs more than the original drives retail price.

Some people try to fix broken drives by <u>deleting some important lists</u> stored in that reserved drive area. The **G-list and p-list** are important lists that help the hard drive avoid bad or worn data areas. Hence, the drive creates its own map of usable area by referring to these 2 lists. If you delete these 2 drives you *create unnecessary mayhem* on your drive.

If the pins on the hard drive **connection port** are damaged then you might have to **replace the entire PCB**. In some cases, you can solder <u>temporary external connections</u> so that the data can be copied onto a new drive. This is definitely <u>not permanent</u> way to repair a damaged hard drive. It is **not a good idea** to open a hard drive <u>without using a laminar-flow work bench</u> or a <u>full-size clean room</u>. Some people believe they can fix a drive by opening the case and *moving the discs back and forth*. This kind of DIY activities **just mess up** people's chance to get data back.

I do need to **crush one misconception** that has been bothering me and many other of my professional DR colleagues in other companies worldwide: People think that if their desk or *kitchen is a clean place to open a drive* then you are absolutely wrong. I have a device I can run for 24 hours in that room. You would be shocked to see the stuff flying in your room while you presume to be **breathing clean ear**. It **is really ghastly what then accumulates** after a day in the air purifier.

It is not unusual for data recovery firms to charge an additional decontamination fee as these unprofessionally opened drives often have accumulated particles on the discs that can kill new parts. These fees can be somewhere between $150 - $600 per disc on average and depending on the region where the laboratory is based. These fees have to be paid irrelevant of the outcome of a data recovery attempt. This is due to the fact that the experts need to commit a lot of time to try to cleanse each disc and heads with special liquids.

Some DR Experts have been experimenting with a process to clean drives in a special liquid bath and using highly toxic gases (e.g., research as part of a JV with a local university in Japan) to carefully dry the surface of the drives without having to dismantle the drives. Unfortunately, these methods have proven to be very costly and pose sever health risks for technicians. It will take further research till a reliable solution has been developed.

1.1.2 Flash memory and their technical issues

You might have read the word "flash device" or "flash memory" in multiple publications. Let me explain what that is actually referring to. Flash devices include USB pend drives, SD memory cards, compact flash cards, and SSD drives (which we handle in a separate chapter of this book).

In recent years it became known that flash memory gradually loses memory areas as they experience a sort of wear. Until recent years manufacturers and general knowledge was that these dying areas become useless due to regularly having to store new information during a **write to memory process**.

Therefor **manufacturers designed algorithms** inside the controllers of these flash devices **to expand the life span of each memory cell** by theoretically distributing the usage evenly among all cells. Some manufacturers false **believed that using encryption** would be a far better method than using a distribution method (algorithm). That is partly why some **very expensive** and highly branded **products died faster** than the cheaper devices of no name brands, which did not use encryption.

So **how is data stored** in a cell? Imagine each cell to be like a soccer goal with a ball inside it. The ball is either stuck to the goal post or hovering inside the goal or the ball is not there at all. These are the **3 possible stages of information stored** in a cell. The ball is representing an electron. The goal is the memory **cell gutter**. We either have a **0 or 1** depending on <u>where the electron is</u>. If there is no electron then the cell <u>has no information</u> and hence, **no recollection of ever having information stored** in it.

People often believe that a flash drive is identical to a traditional hard drive using discs to store data. Memory chips are not directly sensitive to being dropped but they don't take it easily when they are exposed to bending pressure, heat and power surges. Besides that, a flash drive has 3 stages of data while usually a hard drive only has zeros or nulls. Just looking at the different types of flash memory devices we need to be aware that they not only have <u>different casings and connectors</u> but also design purposes. In the following picture you will see a **SxS** card that is used in **professional TV station cameras**. These cards easily cost $500 and more. In order to read the data, you need special equipment. Once they are "broken" you need to **unsolder the chips** and try to recover the data. If you do this the wrong way, you will kill the memory chips and <u>render the data useless</u>.

Photo: SXS Memory Card for Professional Studio Cameras

Any drive that is plugged into a connector or pushed into an adapter's slot is going to be exposed to some sort of discomforting pressure. Hereby the memory card may be **bent or squeezed** a little too much for the devices comfort. That can start off a process of gradual or immediate failure. In some cases, people even manage to **cause a short circuit** by bending pins or crushing connectors in an awkward manner.

There also known cases where being charged up with an **electric charge** can cause a memory device to be damaged when being connected with a separate source of power (e.g., pushed into the notebooks SD card reader or PCI slot). In recent years notebook manufacturers **have increased the safety of their products** so that a **potential power surge** coming from a faulty USB device can't kill the notebook nor other connected devices. Such power surges can even kill a brand-new USB pen drive on the first event of plugging it into the USB connector of a desktop computer.

PS: There is a special *USB killer pen drive* for testing if a USB device port of a notebook has the required power surge protection.

If a user aggressively pulls out a flash device from the computer's connection port it can lead to the device **being bent or slightly crushed** without the user seeing any outside damage. When you look at it using a special microscope you **see the cracks**.

I once got a USB pen drive that had been run over by a bulldozer on a construction site. A pure glance you could not see any damage but under the microscope you could see how each of the 2 chips were bend in the opposite direction as each chip had been soldered onto the PCB on both sides. The data was unrecoverable at that time.

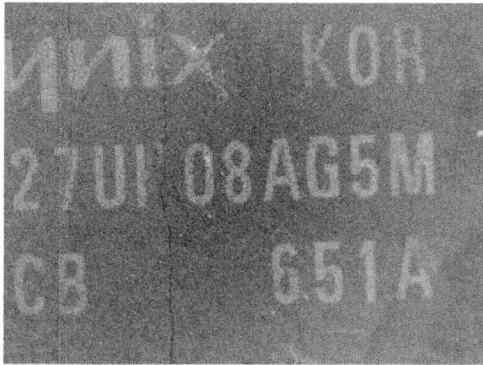
Photo: Chip cracked by bulldozer

If we are lucky by not getting the memory chips cracked then what is actually getting damaged? Usually this is some **controller chip** or transistor or capacitor (Wikipedia, 2011). Following photo shows a professional SXS card having to be opened for a chipoff recovery.

Photo: The inside of a SXS Memory card as used in TV Stations

You might wonder why MS Windows asks you to **release a USB device** or memory card before actually pulling it out of the connection port. By doing this inside windows you tell the operating system (OS) to stop communicating with that device. If you do not release the item, it could be that the **OS is writing information** onto the memory chip at the time you decide to pull the device out of your port slot.

This could **mess up the device's partition table** and cause logical errors. Windows has *built-in repair tools* for such problems but you **cannot count on** the tools actually getting the job done <u>without causing even more problems</u>.

There are multiple free or cheap tools to recover the data. Unfortunately, most users utilize these tools cause severe damage to their healthy files. They try multiple things until a professional DR expert only finds a lot of garbage on the device. Do you think low temperatures can kill your data? Also, heat can damage your devices additional damage and thereby render the memory chips useless. That is why laboratories **use prescribed temperatures** to either <u>cool off chips or warm them up</u> when they need to cause an intended reaction inside the chips. Chips must also be removed from a PCB by using the right tools and heating methods.

There are **2 types** of memory chips. Most often you would find **TPOS** chips with pins on both short ends. As memory capacity is growing manufacturers go towards using BGA chips (Ball Grid Array).

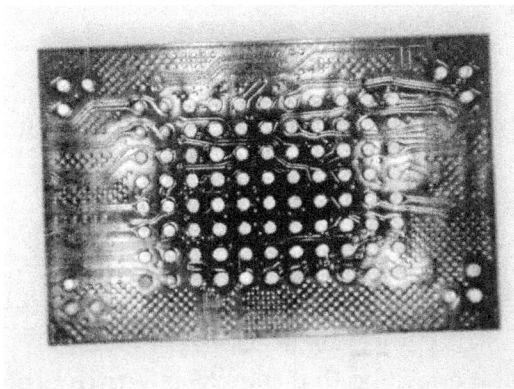

Photo: Bottom side of a BGA Chip

The problem with BGA chips is that due to the **multiple soldering connections** between PCB and the chip can become a risk for the person who is trying to detach the chip from the PCB. If the unsoldering is done *incorrectly*, then the chip will most likely **suffer internal tear**. Such wrong rescue attempts can kill the chip. For such BGA chips an expert will prefer to use a **rework station**. Of course, you can use a **heat gun** but that is not really very safe.

As you will see from the pictures a BGA has many small solder balls attached to the chip's connection pads (in later chapter you can see the pads under a microscope).

So, recovering data from such flash devices requires **special soldering equipment** and methods to remove the chip from the PCB. Once the chip is unsoldered and has been *properly cleaned* you will need to reach the bits stored in that chip. For that you also need specialized equipment and the necessary knowledge to turn a lot of garbage data into useful files by applying the correct reverse engineered algorithms. In the section *"data recovery tools"* I will be listing the equipment and explaining what the differences are.

Such kind of data extraction knowledge is also used for digital forensics. As you read on, you will get a better understanding that this kind of work is often exaggerated by Hollywood's NCIS movies and some dubious market participants. In some criminal cases suspects try to destroy their smartphones, USB pen drives and SSD drives just to prevent the police laboratory from extracting the evidence that will lead to a conviction.

Nevertheless, you do need some good processing power to handle some of the computing when you are trying to reengineer and recover data from damaged flash devices as *algorithms* and desired data can be quite vast. Besides, the variations of memory chips and controller chips make it often time consuming to reengineer the way the controller stored the data on the chip. Not every chip on the market has the same algorithm.

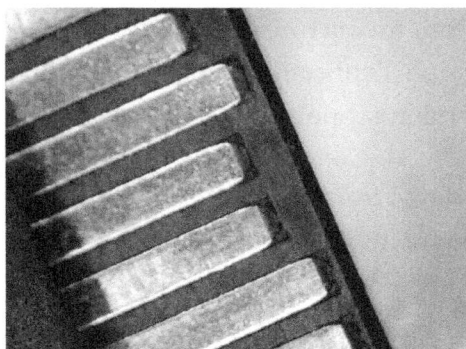

Photo: Contact pins on a USB pen drive

As mentioned before, you will also find flash memory inside photo cards you use in your digital cameras and smartphones. The different types of memory cards available for digital cameras are quite vast. Same applies also for the available range of product quality and reliability.

The **undeniable factor** that **most often causes** an unreversible data loss is due to consumers and IT experts trying to recover data by **applying wrong methods** to rescue their data. After such attempts we often find that data has been *damaged so intensively* that there can't be any recovery done that will lead to good files. This kind of silly tampering just doesn't make any sense.

So often data recovery experts exchange the craziest stories where people have gone to unbelievable length just to try *not to spend money*. Once they have messed up everything they go to a lab and **deny having done any modifications**. Later on, they confess having messed the system up once they are devastated by the realization, **they destroyed their own data**.

By the way, there is a multitude of other popular devices that are now using flash memory to replace old storage methods. Just look at new Dictaphones, MP3 players, PBX, Desk phones, hearing aids, aviation flight recorders and many other devices.

1.2 Organisational Causes of Data Loss

Sometimes companies lose their data due to the way their organisation has chosen to handle data and the infrastructure it put in place. Often **decision makers do not understand** the implications of their chosen level of security. Therefore, they underestimate the risks they are forcing their business to be exposed to.

1.2.1 Insufficient precautions

Most often we find that organisations have not made the effort to implement precautions that are absolutely necessary to protect the organisation from a **crippling system failure**. Unfortunately, some decision makers prefer to cut their data security costs by removing backup systems and power surge security. When the inevitable failure occurs, the organisation is then driven into oblivion by this short-sighted planning.

Upon such misled activities employees attempt to do a DIY job on the broken devices. Some of them are driven by the **hope of a promotion** and eventually maximize the damage for the organisation. They attempt multiple kinds of repair jobs. If they all don't result in a reinstatement of the normal situation, they inevitable decide to consult a true expert who then sees no other option than to declare the data as lost for ever.

Instead of behaving like true gentlemen they revert to blaming the expert for their own incompetence and greed. Looking at their misguided management you will recognize that for less than the price of a bicycle that organisation could have protected itself while saved itself the money they had to pour out on recovering the left overs of their unprofessional attempt at doing the job themselves.

Arguing that you cannot protect yourself against systems failures is not an acceptable excuse for not spending any money on data security. I once got told by a big law firm, that it is not worth paying for data security as you cannot protect the business 100% of the time. As you can imagine, I definitely would not lay my business secrets in this lawyers' hands as otherwise I may have to expect losing it.

On the other hand, if you do **invest sensibly in data security** you can save a lot of money. It can even be **user friendly and uncomplicated**. You **do not need to overdo** it. Just be smart and look at where you might be in danger of getting hurt. Try to **limit the risks** and the damages. Then look at what would be the best reaction if a system did fail. **Plan ahead** and write a **standard operations procedure manual**. You can even stick it to the door or even on every rack cabinet door.

1.2.2 Silly Cost Cutting

,As previously mentioned, cost cutting and false belief of one's own capabilities at solving a damaged system problem often leads to sever escalation of the situation. This cost cutting not only **motivates people** to not buy backup systems or continue to use worn out backup tapes or do other crazy stuff. When you ask a data recovery expert about some of the crazy stuff people do not to protect their data you would be utterly shocked.

When I remember the odd evenings, I would gather with fellow DR experts from other countries after a long training day. It definitely was quite a jolly and sometimes very mellow atmosphere. Learning about all sorts of **new complexities in data recovery** does require some kind of distraction to stop the mind going around all those bits and bytes. Eventually the conversation reminds me a little bit of seamen gathering at a pub.

Just think of those users who try to recover their data by watching YouTube videos. They then **download free software** and **copy badly extracted files** directly back onto the drive where the healthy data is residing. As a result, they damage the good data. Because that dissatisfies them, they get more free software and do the same action over and over again. Then after days they recognize that they are getting nowhere. So, they go to a data recovery company.

Once the expert either has been told what stupid stuff the user has done to his device, he will recognize by years of experience, that he might be wasting his time with this case. If you do put the time and energy into such **self-sabotaged cases,** you **keep getting out totally shredded data**. It can be frustrating to put hours into that case just to recognize your chances of success were already gone by the time the user decided to go to a professional.

Some people down know that a recovery-cd puts an image on top of the original data. The image placed on the drive overwrites the logical data that told us where the files are you need back. Thereby you also loose the logical structure that user see as folder structure.

This often requires to use a raw data recovery to move like a trawler and fish the files without knowing their file names, and original logical organisation. Not many people enjoy <u>opening thousands of word files</u> to figure out **which file belongs into which folder** and subject matter. The time they waste after such recovery CD jobs costs them more than if they had asked a professional right after losing the data in the first place.

Some organisation think it is ok to save money by not training their computer department staff. They **should be grateful** that these computer nerds are hungry to learn new knowledge. Most people are jolly by the time they leave school hoping they will never again have to learn a painful subject. When I think of the months and multiple certifications I used to learn for during my time in corporate. I paid my own trainings and exam fees. No one gave me time off in corporate to learn for the exams. Only mad dogs apparently enjoy learning new crazy computer stuff. Unfortunately, even some heads of IT departments think it is good standard behaviour to <u>keep computer people from learning new knowledge and skills</u>.

I am very **grateful to Microsoft** for so much good training I received as I could fix most of my server failures myself. Well, **15 certifications** must be good for something? Don't you think?!

It is by far better to be cautious when your system reports a system failure or abnormal system behaviour. Some organisations also like sending newsletters to staff <u>telling them about data protection laws and responsibilities</u>. Why do they keep <u>forgetting</u> to **tell people what to do** if something goes wrong to solve the problem? Some of the authors of these compliance related newsletters are deep in love with laws and regulations.

Unfortunately, the legal department and Head of HR have no idea how to really get their systems back up running. Just to make matters worse, the controllers jump into the scene from the side, objecting to <u>spending money on quality systems</u>. They are experts in telling people off when they want to invest in safety or consider to get advice from expert companies. Once the system fails it is not their fault. The IT guys broke the system. Because they IT guys can't handle the situation, they prefer to outsource the work to some company in India. Next time your server breaks, be patient as travel is a time consumer. The visa for the technician in Kerala is waiting to be approved.

So how could you reduce your exposure while being soft on your spending? Provide simple and understandable information to workers what to do when a system fails. Tell them who to contact and what definitely not to do (e.g., attempt a DIY job). You can even use colourful PowerPoint diagrams and workflow maps. Also respect the advice from a junior staff member who has had the proper training elsewhere. Some people think just because they have a master's degree that they are entitled to destroy the company's data with their ill driven ego. I have seen more competent young men and women who could fix a system without having studied at university. Having the right training costs money but it will definitely safe many jobs and a fortune to the owners of the business.

Regarding those data privacy sheets employees are regularly told to sign even if the content <u>could not be understood by a rocket scientist</u>: This is a waste of your employer's money as you are **not improving data security** nor generating any contribution to the organisation's profitability. These pointless circulating forms remind me a little of the old TV series *"Are you being served"*. Keep the data privacy and security training in a way that even the simplest human will understand the risks to everybody should ignorance prevail in a situation of failure. Tell them what would be a sensible way to look at the situation.

I personally prefer to **leave out all these laws and regulatory junk** as people cannot make sense of it unless they have studied law in the first place. My experience shows that by **telling people a story** they **can relate to** what I am actually trying to get them to understand. In some cases, I will shock them with what happens when you do not react cautiously and ask for help from those who are truly qualified to investigate the issue in the system.

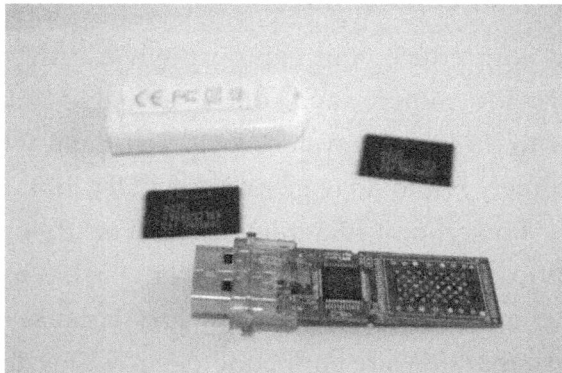

Photo: USB pen drive with 2 memory chips

Asking questions later on gives me an insight if the penny has dropped with people. They then have definitely **understood the seriousness of the subject** and know how to behave in such unpleasant situations. They no longer run around like headless chickens. When such a situation arises, they behave like gentlemen and ladies should do. They make you very proud of them, when you notice they have embraced your educative stories. That is when you have truly mastered cost cutting in the way it should be done by intelligent people.

1.3   Device-specific Reasons for Failure

In order to better understand why some devices are failing more or less often, I would like to provide you a better understanding of these products. Besides **accidents, material wear and other causes of damage** to a device there is also an element which is not talked about that often. This last cause of device failure is known as the planned obsolescence of products. I will be handling this delicate subject in a later chapter.

As you have read in previous sections of this book there are some technical and organisational (or human) reasons for devices and systems failing. This system outage leads to the need for data recovery in order to **avoid permanent data loss**. As we go deeper into each storage technology you will recognize that there are some limitations to the longevity of storage. Technology will never be perfect as it is made by humans who themselves are not perfect, either.

1.3.1 Hard Drive

A traditional hard drive will have mechanical and electronical parts inside that can be damaged by sudden movements or malfunction. Even magnetic influences can pose a risk to the drive. Hence, companies should avoid exposing their equipment to **excessive electro-magnetic waves** (ESD). According to a Swedish regulation a person's work environment should not be exposed to values above 0.2 micro tesla (=mu). As a level of 0.3mu a conventional desktop screen (like you had in the 90ties) would flicker. Most people living beside high-speed train tracks are not aware of the magnetic fields they are being exposed to when the wiring above the tracks is not well adjusted. Even 1km away studies have shown that they could measure 2mu inside an office building.

Let me highlight the key parts of a hard drive and how they could suffer:

In some countries people like to call the „**Actuator**" (1) the reading arm or something similar. This sort of arm holds the heads and could be described more like a fork as when you have several heads on that arm you will see several "spikes" forming a fork. This fork or actuator hovers above the surface of the **rotating disks** (2). As mentioned, at each tip of that actuators spikes you will find that on both sides of the spikes are little boxes. These boxes as in fact the heads (8) of the drive.

If you drop the drive by mistake the **heads** (8) will hit on the surface (2) of the drive and the spikes of the actuator (1) would often be bent. As people start up the drive the damaged heads create scratches and leave a residue like ashes. That creates dirt on the surface thereby reducing a drives ability to read the drive. Experts remove the damaged actuator, clean the surface and insert a new compatible actuator with healthy heads.

Photo: Parts of a hard drive

1) Actuator
2) Disc surface
3) Motor
4) Controller
5) Filter
6) SATA Port
7) Blocker
8) Heads
9) Ramp

As heads scratch or jump on the surface they can cause small sparks, which causes additional damage to the heads and the vulnerable surface. Inside the drive is a particle filter (5) that would usually suck in all the regular dust or dirt that is produced by a drive. When the sparks occur, the dirt will eventually be sucked into the filter. In a few cases one then needs to remove the filter or even replace it just to recover the data without getting into additional problems. As you look at the area surrounding the actuator you will notice a white plastic part called the **blocker** (7). This part ensures that the discs are generating sufficient airflow for the heads (8) to hover safely above the surface without touching it. Once the blocker releases the **actuator** (1) it moves across the disk and lets the arms start reading the disks. If the **motor** (3) or the **motor IC** on the PCB is faulty then that can also cause dangerous malfunctions.

The SATA Ports and the power connections are seldom the cause of a drive failing. A greater risk exists if the PCB has a USB port soldered on it, as users can easily break it off by accident. The PCB is an additional complex part belonging to the hard drive and may suffer a variety of damages. A power surge can damage the 5V and 12V fuses as well as make the **motor IC crack**.

Photo: Heads parked on the (orange) ramp

1.3.2 USB Hard Drive

Traditional 3.5in USB hard drives have an additional **USB to SATA PCB** (2) attached to the drive's main PCB. The smaller 2.5 and 1.8 drives usually have a USB port directly on the main PCB. Only older drives and very cheap models still use the additional USB2SATA adapters.

1.3.3 Network Array Storage (NAS) Drives

If you are using a storage system that can be reached over your local network then you will be using a NAS. These NAS Systems run on Linux or Windows Home Server operating system. A NAS can hold 1 or more drives in its chasey. You will most often encounter systems with 2, 4, 5 or 6 bays. Don't be mistaken to believe it will replace your professional server. These systems often fail when continuously run for years on a 24x7. The **damage caused by users** trying to fix their NAS most often causes further damage. They do stuff that is unbelievable. Thereby, they damage the partition data or even totally destroy their own data by putting drives with other data into the existing bays.

People tend to **misunderstand the manuals** and apply commands that do exactly the opposite of what they intended to do. The other nice one is, **misunderstanding the manufacturer's support** team and not telling the hotline staff the true situation. Thereby, the support engineers hand out a repair manual that entices the user to force the drives to perform actions the drives are no longer fit to do. That damages the data and potentially scratches off all the surface on the drives. Having a RAID setting does not protect your data from wrong ways of attempting to fix a NAS.

Too often you see that users force a Raid rebuild command and when the system notices its running against issues, it will stop. The user then again and again **initiates the rebuild command**. That eventually makes a terrible mess in the Raid partitions and corrupts the data.

People who buy a NAS think they are now safe from data loss. Because they don't do their homework, their NAS remains a potential havoc. They need to **protect it against a power surge** and water damage. Even a NAS should be regularly backed up to a 3rd party drive. The manufacturers often provide at the back of the encasement fast USB ports. Check the manual before you attach a USB drive!

This is why some corporate clients ask us to advise them on where their data centres might lack security in regards to protecting their storage systems. It definitely pays off for these clients as a power failure in cities and even ransom attacks are a potential threat to any business around the world.

1.3.4 RAID Systems

Depending on the capabilities and settings of a RAID controller you will have access to a variety of RAID configurations. Before setting up a new Server you need to consider what the individual sections of the system have to do and **what risks may appear**. Choose wisely how you build the RAID structures. There are even workstations that support RAID 0 or 1.

Depending on the raid controller you have chosen to use, you will have a set of configurable raid versions available. Choose wisely. Most controllers are capable of Raid 0 and Raid 1. As soon as you can **attach 4 or more drives** you should find at least a **Raid 5 option**. Following short list will give you a brief idea what the different raid versions have to offer:

Raid 0 creates a large storage area spanning over several drives. You get simplicity and speed at the cost of potential data loss should one drive get damaged or be destroyed. There is no redundancy and no protection against failure.

Raid 1 is a group of mirrored drives. If your system has 2 drives built in, it will write the data simultaneously onto both drives. This creates an identical copy. If 1 drive fails, you still have 1 copy accessible. This does not protect against accidental deletion or malicious attacks (e.g., ransomware)

Raid 2 is the extension of the raid 1 concept. This version has been given a parity section using the "Hamming-Code" to provide redundancy. This is a bit stripe technology.

Raid 3 has a Bit-Stripe with dedicated parity information.

Raid 4 uses block level stripes with dedicated information.

Raid 5 uses block level stripes with distributed information. If a NAS or server only has 4 drives with this raid type then you can only afford to lose 1 drive. Loose a second drive and you might be screwed, should one of both failed drives be unrecoverable. Ideally, a professional setup should include a minimum of 5 drives in a raid 5 constellation.

Raid 6 uses block level stripes with double distributed information.

Hybrid Raid Concepts:

Raid 0+1 uses a straight number of hard drives in order to mirror striped drives. This offers a higher protection against data loss but increases the complexity for recovery depending on the damage on your drives.

Raid 1+0 mirrors drives and distributes the mirrored data across stripes. As long a mirror does not lose all its stripes on one disc there is a higher data loss protection. This scenario is prone to wrong repair attempts by novice users.

Raid 5+3 is a mirrored set of block level stripes with distributed parity Information.

Some manufacturers use their very own raid concepts that make them presumably safer but also more difficult to recover. Professional raid tools have continued to improve helping data recovery experts waste less time on trying to figure out how the system was really configured. The problem often arises when raid systems have some minute modifications that are not typical.

Raid 50EE is a Raid 0 containing 2 Raid 5EE (5+1+1). This strategy can easily cope with losing 2 drives. If the configuration has a mistake, the data is rendered useless. In a *„degraded mode"*, you can even temporarily continue to work with the system while not having access to 4 drives.

HP's ADG is a special derivate of Raid 6 (Wikipedia, 2012 b).

Therefore, the smart administrator must choose wisely. If not sure, consult first with an expert what is the safest method and how to mitigate any potential risks. Not taking care at this stage of setting up a system is leading directly to data loss.

Even if the administrator has been diligent enough to write down a operational manual, he or she must keep this document up to date. In over 70% of cases data recovery experts have found that the stated raid set up stated by the admin does not match the settings that were actually present in the raid system. As some NAS and servers are not very well maintained in SMEs the risk of data loss is there by far higher than in corporations. Nevertheless, even an IT Director with 1000 information technology specialists can't presume being protected by some heavenly force. Ignorance, arguments and internal discomforts lead to data loss even in multi-national organisations.

It is true that corporations often have larger data centres with great equipment against fire and theft, but even there, mistakes do happen.

They will even use complex disaster scenarios to protect themselves. This will even include a backup data centre that is built into trucks that pull up in an emergency within 24 hours to get the company systems back up running.

1.3.5 SSD Drives

SSD drives are the next generation of flash storage devices that evolved from USB pen drives. Some SSD drives even include SDRAM memory chips to speed up data processing and transition. The SDRAM acts as a cache (Toshiba HG Series). Some SSDs use Single Level Cell (SLC) or multi-level Cell (MLC) technology (Toshiba, 2012).

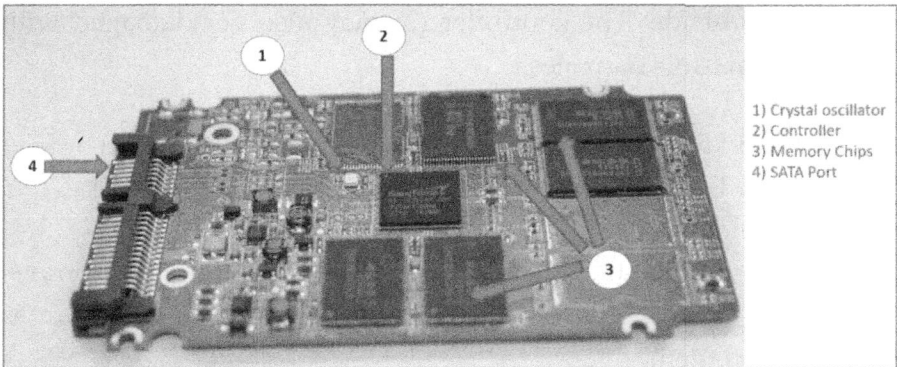

1) Crystal oscillator
2) Controller
3) Memory Chips
4) SATA Port

Photo: PCB of SSD without DRAM

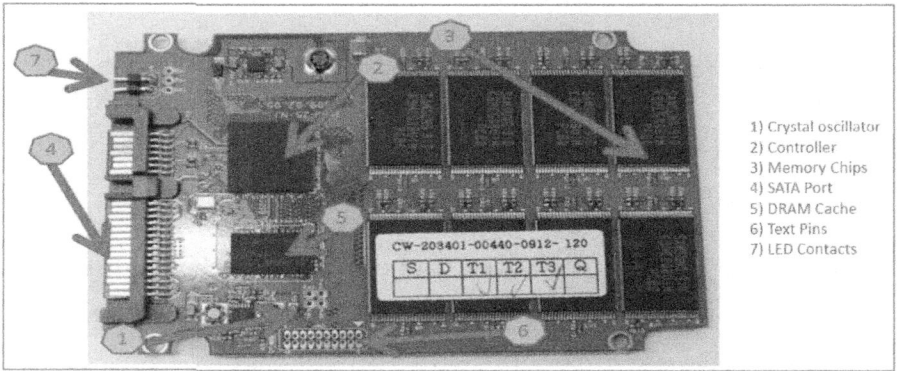

1) Crystal oscillator
2) Controller
3) Memory Chips
4) SATA Port
5) DRAM Cache
6) Text Pins
7) LED Contacts

Photo: PCB of SSD with DRAM

1.3.6 USB Pen Drives

USB pen drives usually have 1 or more memory chips built in. The chips have pins at the sides or ball pads on the surface of the chips bottom side (Wikipedia, 2011).

It can happen that a memory chip (3) gets damaged inside. You will notice cracks on the outside of the casing. Some damages you can't spot from outside. The controller (2) may also get damaged with visible or invisible damages.

You will find more often the USB port wiring (5) getting torn or bent and thereby losing the connection to the printed circuit board.

The crystal oscillators do tend to get damage as users often travel with them around. These are often expose to a lot of pressure as people sit on them.

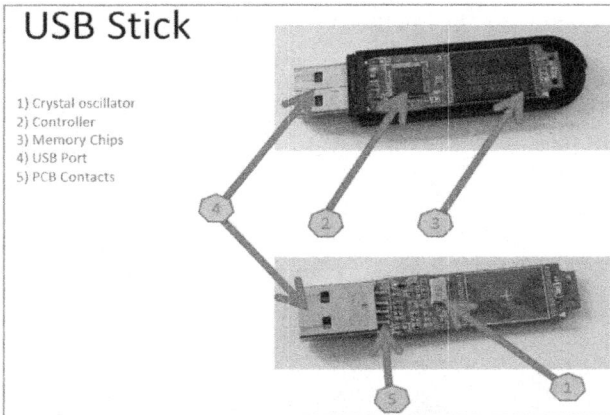
Photo: USB Pen Drive

1.3.7 Memory Cards

You will find that memory cards come in many different formats. As the years passed, we saw some standards disappearing (e.g., xD). The key change in their evolution is their speed and storage capacity. This comes at a significant cost for users. Data los increases rapidly beyond the capacity of 4 GB.

People tend to not take care of the memory cards as they should. The get bend, sat on, overheated or even through around the office like some card game. Even the family pet has enjoyed a bite at the memory card. As these storage devices have a very flat surface design, the memory chips do not have much protection against pressure and mal treatments. This puts controllers and other parts at risk of being damaged, too.

The worst scenario is when a controller is melting. At the very beginning of flash data recovery this kind of scenario created massive problems for data recovery. The manufacturers of the recovery equipment eventually managed to create helpful functionalities to help identify the kind of controller this could have been.

More recent technology developers have gone a new route by **eradicating the dependency on the controller information**. This more advanced strategy requires more complex training and also more time as the newer devices have even greater storage capacity.

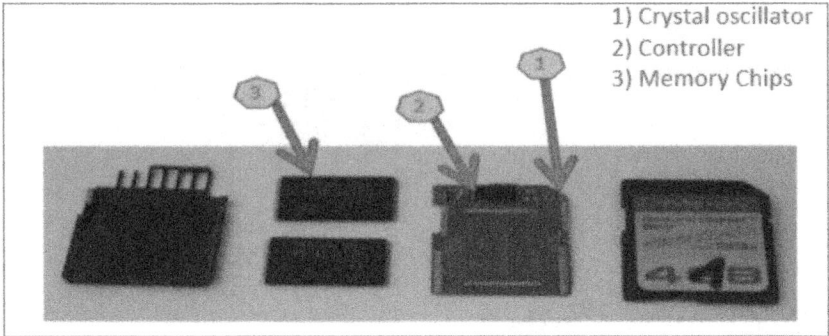

Photo: Parts of a SD Memory Card

A Compact Flash card (CF, CFII) is similar to the SD card.

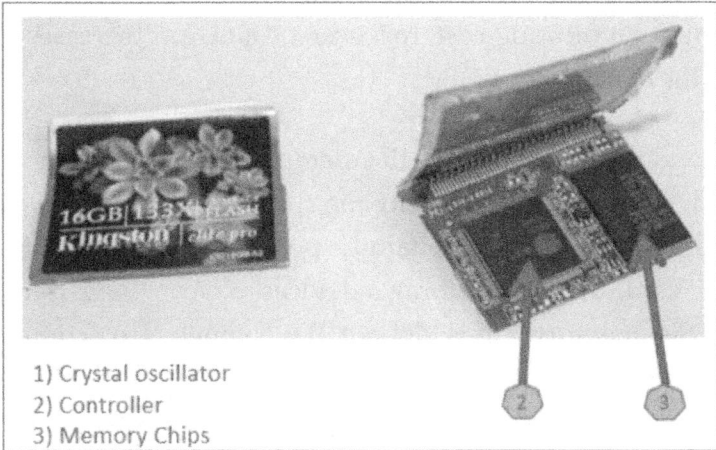

Photo: Parts of a Compact Flash Card

Memory chips in both systems are addressed by the controller in a similar way. CF cards have more space available and are often **more robust due to the tougher casing**.

1.4 Data loss due to sabotage

1.4.1 Ransomware

In 2015-2016 ransomware attacks were at their hight. Files used to be deleted, encrypted or distorted, in order to force the victim to pay a ransom using bitcoin. Recently in 2021 the pandemic allowed attackers to modify their strategies and focus on a new set of victims.

Some attackers used to modify the headers or footers of files in order to render them useless. Once the victim paid the files would be stitched together. This kind of manipulation could be analysed and fixed using our tool *"cryptcleaner"*.

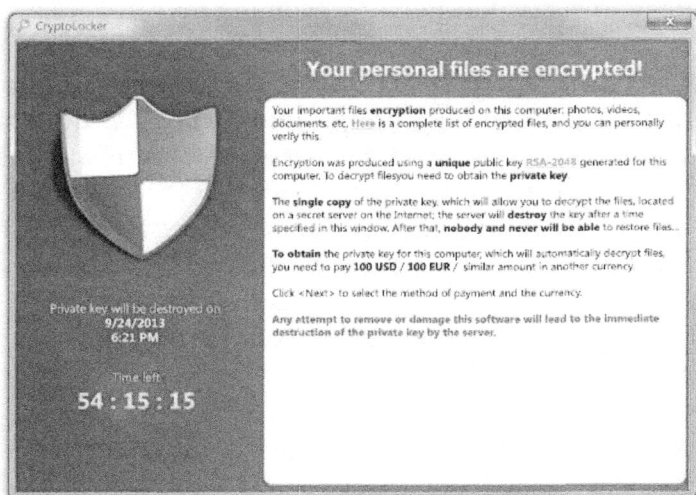

Photo: Screen from a ransom ware attack on a Windows 7

Other attackers focused first on deactivating and disabling the installed antivirus software. They used a vulnerability known as the **4MB tactic** or by filling up the entire C partition with an automated **junk file creating strategy**.

1.4.2 Fax Attacks

The attacker uses the fax protocol to hijack the targeted fax machine. A set of special commands are used to force the fax machine to become remote control and **act as backdoor**.

Multi-function printers can be turned into weapons by applying special fax commands. This danger is existing in many devices from a variety of manufacturers that were sold in Europe. It is possible to include in the fax message a payload that is then **executed in the memory of the fax machine**. A payload is a file or a set of commands that has been hidden inside the message. Depending on the fax machine and the **attack strategy** one can send the entire payload in one message or utilize several messages to transmit the attack system. If a **payload is segmented**, the attacker's program is assembled in the fa machine with every additionally incoming fax.

Once the payload is operational in the machine, the attacker will take over the device and start **exploring the network**. As these modern fax machines are attached to LAN cables and WIFI networks the attacker will be able to connect with a variety of local devices. Based on keywords an attacker's tool will start searching for files and either **intentionally destroy** them or transmit them out side of the victim's network. As the fax machine has access to the internet this transmission of **stolen data** can happen without much resistance. As manufacturers have built in a set of maintenance tools and ports in these devices, the attacker can even use the existing hardware connections to spread to other devices such as other fax machines and computers.

This kind of attack offers additional benefits for the intruder as the fax machines often have limited memory capacity. New faxes and print jobs quickly overwrite the evidence of the attacks. Thereby allowing an attacker even to repeat the attack several time s over a long period of over 6 months without being noticed. This kind of attacks are possible and have been part of several investigations into economic **espionage** and criminal attacks. Small and medium sized businesses in Germany have been victims of such attacks.

3 Data Recovery

Depending on the method of determining the severity of damage, you can either overcomplicate things or make it easy to grasp. I prefer using 4 levels: light, medium, severe, extreme. This principle also helps ranking the associated risks, the to be expected cost of recovery and the potential damage it can cause to the victim.

3.1 Strategic Approach

In order to manage large quantities of data recovery jobs one needs to be well organized. At the beginning you might use very simple method as like writing the name of the client on the device but eventually you will get confused should multiple clients have the same name.

Hence, you need to work on organisational, technical and methodical elements of the business. In order to get this business off the ground you need to invest in marketing, sales and customer service. Ticket systems and ERP software can help stay organized and be professional in the long run. You save time and make more money as you can cope with more incoming requests. As you gradually add staff to your business, you can make sure they keep to your standard operational procedures (SOP).

Thereby you also enable yourself to get access to business statistics. Know how many people are calling you for help and how many are actually delivering their devices to your business. Put that into perspective with your sales and revenue statistics you can eventually see how good you sell. Do not forget to keep an eye of profitability because if the cost keeps rising but you cannot generate a substantial profit then there is something wrong.

3.2 Organisational Planning

You need to be able to track your work. That includes any kind of tasks, communication with clients and suppliers. Even if your business is a 1 man show you still need to take notes.

This is where you eventually develop your own workflow. Know the route a device takes from being delivered to you, to eventually you sending out the offer and it being accepted by the client. The steps of imaging and recovering the data as well as making sure your backup meets the quality standards you have set yourself.

3.2.1 HR Planning

Every business will need humans to get the work done. It doesn't matter if it is only, you or if you have a team of 20 people. Being disorganized is fatal. You have to train people and provide them with SOPs so that they know how and when they have to get something done. Also explain why you want it done this way.

Make sure you invest in training yourself and your crew as this reduces the **risk of failure** and enables you to maximize the internal revenue generation. This also decreases your dependency on a 3rd party doing your job. We used to have a room just a library full of books on hardware, programming, IT security and many other vital topics. Today, we have gone towards a digitalized knowledge database and eBooks. You save space and storage cost in cities where office space is very costly.

Do not ridicule an employee if they are wanting to learn new content. If they are reluctant to educate themselves on the necessary knowledge then you should be aware of future cost due to limited contributions.

3.2.2 Technical Planning

Technology is massively improving and changing. This demands from data recovery experts to keep innovating. That requires regular upgrades to knowhow and technology. This comes with a severe price tag. Your infrastructure needs to improve and be adapted to the technology you are dealing with. As devices get hot, you need to cool them. Some labs use their internal air conditioning and some have to improvise because their building does not offer such conveniences.

It is not enough to rent a garage and do your lab work there. You are handling customer data that is usually sensitive in its nature. Customers are entrusting you with their data. It is true that some customers didn't bother to take care of their equipment and data in the first place, but that does not excuse you from taking care on your side. As your business grows you might decide to upgrade your facility by moving to a better office location.

In times like pandemics, we and our clients are forced to work many days in a home office. That is when we need to evaluate how we can remain professional and alleviate the disadvantages of home office combined with lockdowns. Our intention should be to maintain operational quality and safety. We need to protect customer data and our people. Do not forget protecting also yourself. Insecure work environments lead to accidents or even long-term health issues.

3.3 Technical Possibilities

3.3.1 Drive Analysis

Every new case should start with the drive analysis, after all basic information (customer details and drive identification) has been recorded. Your intention is to speed up your internal processes while identifying the root cause of the issue and the best strategy to recover the data. You need to take into account that a presumably simple case could quickly turn into a problematic job.

A drive that apparently has some simple problem could suddenly suffer a head crash. That would lead to unexpected extra cost and time needed. If you eventually delivered the wrong evaluation to a client that might lead to discomfort and no real understanding for the situation.

As you evaluate the situation you will be using different kind of tools as every case uses different technology for storing and recovering data. Recovering an SSD is done differently from a hard drive with scratching heads. You might even need special equipment (clean room) or spare parts that are not easy to find on the market. Some specialized resellers of donor drives charge autonomous fees for supplying you with the right donor drive. Take that into account when working on the cost estimate for your client.

As you are working on processing the recovery job, you will ned to consider how to standardize and improve the quality of your activities. If you are able to be highly methodical and organized, you could go towards creating a quality management handbook according to the **ISO 9001** standard. There are freelancers who specialize in creating such QM books for companies. I had this done many years ago and it did take quite some of my personal time too. Data recovery is not very well known by most consultants as it is very niche business model.

You might think the opposite is the case, when you look in search engines. The reality is that in most countries very few real data recovery firms exist. All other offers are either resellers or scams.

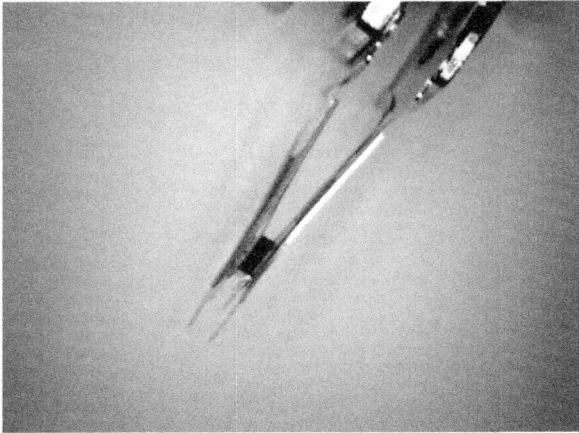

Photo: heads of a hard drive under a microscope

3.3.2 Memory Cards

Memory cards are most often used in digital cameras. The types of cards are vast: SD, MMS, MS Pro, SxS, CompactFlash or xD. These can have **NAND chips, monolithical chips or hybrid** (e.g., MicroSD soldered onto the PCB). Even the number of chips and type of chips can differ very much. The outside casing does not really give much clue about **what is actually inside** until you open the casing. Be careful when opening the casing as people tend to damage the chips using some crazy methods to open the plastic or metal frame.

Cheap memory cards tend to have severe quality issues. Many marketing gifts lead to data loss as **it costs more to print the advertising on the plastic** casing than to produce the electronics inside the device.

Some cheap manufacturers even use glue and melted rubber to make do for their bad casing designs. This just make for a recovery engineer more work to get the PCB out and cleaned.

Sometimes you even **need to apply heat** to get the PCB out. The even nastier side is trying to clean the contacts of chips as the solder is messed up with the plastic glue. Some memory chips have been specially designed against tampering or accidents. They create additional work as you need special workshop style tools to open the protective shields. As this happens you ned to apply a special suction as otherwise the black plastic can damage your lungs or cover the entire surface of the device creating a horrible mess.

Extremely work intensive are BGA-cases, where chips have suffered damage. In such cases both sides of the chip surface have to be heated. The device needs to be **preheated at 150°C** from below and then get additional heat to **take it towards 250°C**. After removing the chip from the PCB, you can carefully begin to clean the chip surface and contacts. You have to do this cleaning as you will need to "**reball**" the chip with new solder balls (*0.4mm diameter*). After the solder has cooled off, you clean the surface and get ready to place the chip into the adapter. The next steps should be a software task, unless there are still some solder issues. Take into consideration, that **corrosion** can damage the pads on the chip. It is very difficult to get that removed without killing the chip itself.

3.3.3 USB Pen Drives

USB pen drives come in all sorts of casings. Some you can push a leaver to get the USB port out of the casing and some you just need to pull the lid off. These drives have a plastic frame that holds the PCB with its USB port on a rail that enables you to push the PCB out of the protective casing so that only the USB connector is visible.

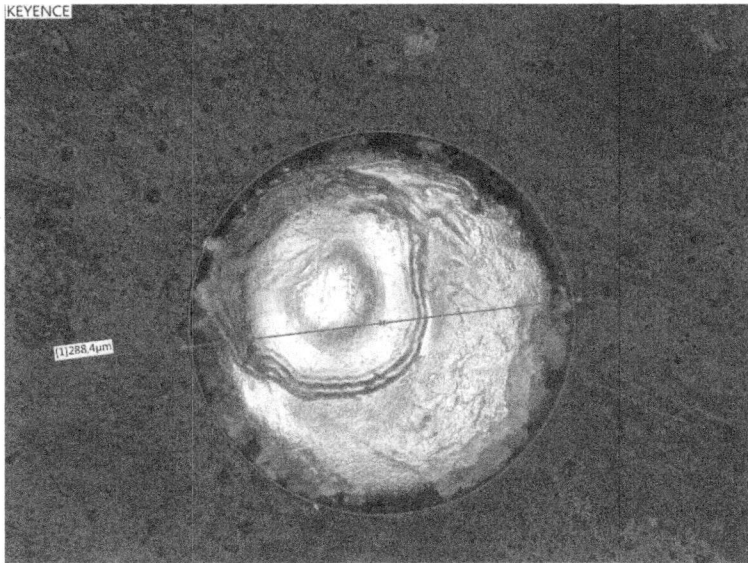

Photo: measuring the diameter (284,4 μm) of a soldering point on a memory chip using a special industrial microscope

Up till 2017 most of the USB Pen drives in *North America and Europe* used to have the classic TSOP chip on the PCB. As capacity demand rises, manufacturers are using BGA chips more often. These BGA related cases require **more sophisticated equipment** in order to recover the data.

Such BGA cases need to get heat applied to the chip and the PCB at different temperature levels. For this you ideally use **hybrid rework stations** as the reduce the risk of losing the chip. They apply the heat to the surface by using an infrared laser and heating wires.

Once you have been able to **softly lift the chip** off the PCB you will need to clean the chip surface. You will need to use a microscope to check if you got all solder off. Using a solder wick of different thickness, you can carefully collect the solder on the solder wick.

The next step will be to read the chip using a special Chip reader and software. This software helps you check which patterns and settings might replicate **the algorithm of the controller** on the PCB. If you do not doo that you only get useless data and in modern cases you don't even get to see any files. Older controllers make this process easier as they are well known and you just need to **apply the existing template** by comparing the print on the controller and your database.

Photo: Residue (from the manufacturer) on the contacts of a memory chip sitting on the PCB of a USB pen drive

Hardware encrypting controllers do not make data recovery impossible. In some cases, it is possible to recover data. The key difficulty for users is to find out if their device is using encryption. Some manufacturers highlight this in the product description but that is not always the case. Traditionally you can expect that a SanDisk device will have a **hardware encrypting controller**. This can present a sever issue when trying to recover data. In very few cases you can recover data even in a chip-off process. If you find that a product claims to use a *SandForce* controller you are definitely going to find it is encrypting the data on the memory chips.

Who does not need to protect the data against unauthorized access does not really need to have such encrypted technology? Nevertheless, the statistics show that there is a marginal difference between encrypted and **non-encrypting devices** when they fail. The key risk of losing data is based on the way people use their devices. Even manufacturers such as **Kingston and Intel offer encrypting storage devices**. We have tested several of these encrypting devices to see if they are able to **prohibit unauthorized access**. If someone can't access the data by guessing your password, then they usually would have to access the data by extracting the data from the memory while bypassing the controller. Your data is presumably safe unless there is some unknown backdoor.

3.3.4 USB Memory Cards

Some companies like to hand out their marketing and press material on memory cards. Unfortunately, some people reuse them for storing critical data. When these devices fail, the cost is way beyond what the device is worth. The shock of the users is understandably severe. Such cheaply manufactured memory devices are absolutely no place to store data of importance. It is highly advisable for IT security staff to make users aware of the risks involved using such devices. The risk of total data loss is substantial!

Some companies want to make sure their IT is well equipped and trained to handle severe crisis. This is where IT audits are a great help to identify shortcomings and prevent severe damage to the business. Following the standards of **ISACA** (= *Information Systems Audit and Control Association*) is a good approach. This is where external data centre consultants help mitigate risks to reputation, infrastructure and workforce (Cannon, 2011).

Some people want to blame the company that gave them the memory device. The fact that the user changed the usage purpose of the device is one of the core reasons why only the user is to blame. The user has to cover the expense of recovering the data in a professional data recovery lab. Furthermore, the IT department needs to know what devices are being used in the company network. Such devices can also lead to other kinds of security risks. What is the key differentiation of USB memory cards and that of regular USB memory devices? The memory card has to be extremely compact. This leads to a **monolithic** design. A USB-pen drive has lots of space for memory chips and its controller.

3.3.5 Hard Drives

Mechanical hard drives are very different from SSD drives. That is why both types of drives tend to suffer a data loss to very different reasons. Users believe that switching to an SSD will remove the risk of losing data completely. An SSD will put you at a higher risk. Why? I will explain in the SSD section.

Photo: Hard drive heads using special industrial microscope.
Image taken 2016 in our laboratory.

Mechanical hard drives need protection against sudden movements as they are prone to getting damaged by sudden impact. They do not like being moved around while they are reading disks.

Following list highlights the type of events that will lead to a hard drive eventually or rapidly failing:

- Being dropped, hitting something or being caught in mid air
- Sitting on your desk and being pulled forward as the rubber feet of the casing rattles on the desk surface
- Being inside a notebook that is being hit by an angry person
- Being badly packed for a rough transport
- Power surge due to lightning
- getting the wrong power adapter attached
- Being sat on or something heavy squeezing it

3.3.6 SSD Drives

Modern SSD drives are not really affected by being dropped. Of course, they do not like being squeezed or bent. They permanent system failures are due to following occurrences:

- Electromagnetic disturbances
- Power surge
- Wrong wiring
- Incompatibility with computer hardware
- pressure being applied to outer casing
- Severe temperature changes
- Temperature under 1°C
- Material fatigue
- Cheap components
- Wrong commands by older OS
- And other unknown causes

Don't rely on a SSD excusing you for not doing your regular backups. Data loss can occur also with an SSD drive! As more users switch to SSD drives to enjoy superior speed they are also exposed to other kinds of risks.

If a SSD fails one usually will need to dismantle the drive. Some cases do not require this hardcore work. If the Controller of the SSD is no longer functioning properly, then you have to go deep. This will require substantial memory capacity in a data recovery computer.

3.3.7 Raid Systems

With a raid setup one usually tries to mitigate the risk of a failing hard drive. The higher the raid number the better the safety will be? Currently you will find *Raid Version 0, 1, 4, 5, 6, 10, 20, 60* in many data centres. Cluster and „**Cloud Computing**"? This technology has a very different and further advanced strategy to ensure data loss is avoided.

3.3.8 Cell phones and Smartphones

What can you do if your smartphone or traditional cell phone dies on you? There are usually a lot of images or important information stored on them. Some on can use JTG but if things are really bad you have to opt for Chip-off.

What really increases the damage? Some users tend to tr to fix their devices by simply restarting their phone. If there is water damage then that can exponentially increase the damage. In such cases, the humidity can cause a power surge and damaging some very sensitive components.

Some users seem to believe that putting the device in an oven at 50°C will fix the issue. Just try to handle a lot of melted plastic. This kind of madness just increase the cost and risk of permanent data loss. A more smoothening approach is to use rice and specialized chemicals. You need to remove the humidity as best as possible. Also try to remove any kind of dirt that can lead to additional system failure. This kind of situations can require a lot of work in a data recovery laboratory. Not every situation is problematic.

Sometimes one can use specialized adapters and wiring to extract the data should the device be able to boot up. If this is impossible, one will need to remove the memory chip from the phone's PCB. This takes time as first you have to remove lots of metal and plastic components that are covering the key areas you need to get to. Once you got to the PCB and nothing is obstructing you from safely accessing the chip, then it's necessary to heat up the PCB with a special heating equipment at a temperature fitting to that particular device.

Photo: PCB of a Smartphone with protected memory chips

Once you have removed the chip from the PCB you will need to examine it under a special microscope. You need to clean the surface of any solder residue and repeat this cleaning job until the chip is in a usable state. Then you can place it into a chip reader (see devices in later chapter) and use its software to image the date on the chip. If the device has had quite some damage you will have to expect a repeated reading as a necessary precaution.

Photo: Smartphone with damage from violent person trying to destroy evidence

In many cases these devices have a lot important data of CEOs and sales staff. They are important for the business client and that is why they are often willing to invest in the costly data recovery process.

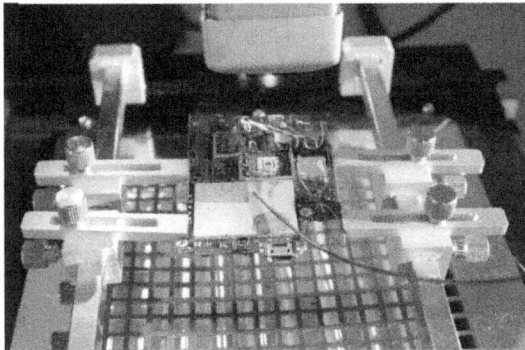

Photo: Smartphone PCB after removing the chip needed for data recovery

Consumers are less likely going to spend money on a smartphone chip-off unless they forgot to store their data in the cloud. Most phone repair shops can fix the typical damaged display or plugs. Even changing the battery is quite easy for most phones. Getting access to the data inside is not something a phone repair shop should attempt as they might destroy the memory chips.

Users should explore methods to backup their data. There are tools that just cost $15 to backup even large devices like an iPhone 11 with 128GB capacity. Companies have quite a different problem to solve. If they have no standard way of protecting the data on smartphone devices, they are being exposed to IT security risks. Device management solutions are a great help. Unfortunately, many businesses are not well equipped to protect themselves against cyber threats and espionage. Newer tactics use SMS and email to hijack smartphones and use them as trojans in corporate networks.

3.3.9 Additions to this book

As time has progressed since writing the very first edition of this book in 2011 technology and research has evolved. I would like to show you some of our research into what causes damage and prevents a successful data recovery.

As more manufacturers use **epoxide and silicone** to protect their chips on the PCB against sudden drops and overly being put under pressure, they are increasing the workload on labs. If you heat up epoxide it becomes like a glibber mass like a chewing gum. Just think of that undesirable gum that likes sticking to your shoes if you accidentally step on in in the road.

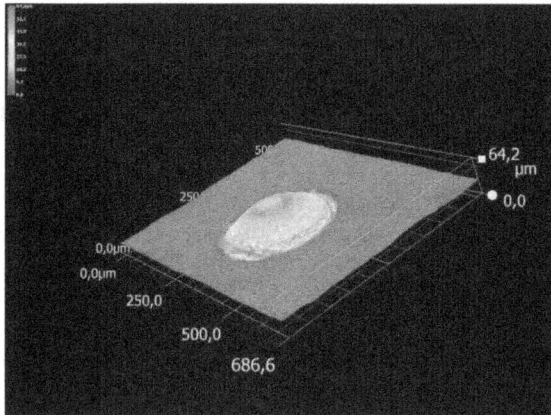

Photo: Measuring the hight of tiny soldering points on a
Smartphone memory chip

If small elements of Epoxide of the size of 10 - 18 (mu) then you have a nasty issue to handle.

3.3.9.1   Can such problems be solved easily?

A smartphone is often damaged by water, pressure, being dropped or being severely destroyed by impact. This leads to cracks in the chip surface. Some of these internal problems can be overcome using a special freezing method. This does not work for eMMC chips. Using the 1000X high resolution industrial microscope you can recognize how soldering have a beneficial or problematic effect on memory chips. An ideal solder ball with a hight of 30 (mu) is a perfect connector. Using standard microscopes, you cannot see this kind of detail.

3.3.9.2   Who needs complex data recoveries?

In digital forensics such cases often require chip-off. The challenges of such an assignment shouldn't be underestimated.

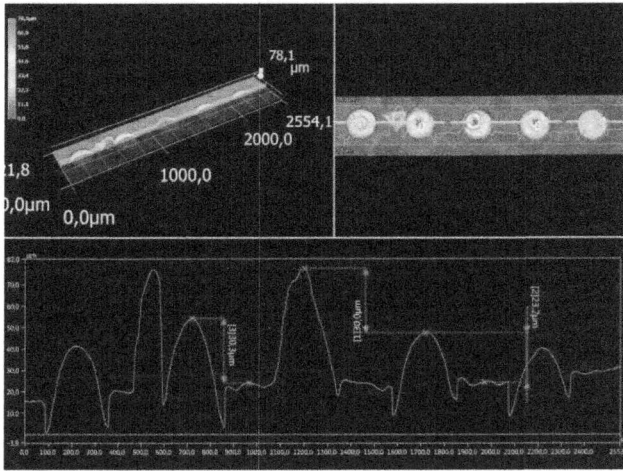

Photo: Comparing highs of 5 neighbouring solder points in a chip

The range of eMMC chip includes standard memory chips and hybrid chips with integrated RAM. Most manufacturers are using eMMC chips now. As they scale their technology, they are adopting the hybrid eMMC chip.

3.3.9.3   How difficult is it to recognize such issues?

Using such expensive microscopes help in research. The daily challenge of data recovery experts is to predominantly extract data and not research the cause of failure. Hence, you will not necessarily encounter such a device that costs well above a 5-figure amount. Engineers are busy enough **trying to reengineer how the controller stored the data** on the chip. This is not always a straight forward job that is completed by pressing a button. This task can take up hours or weeks. When it comes to a forensic case of high priority then the objective is not to recover beautiful pictures but to access evidence that provides insights into what happened and what potentially might be the next move.

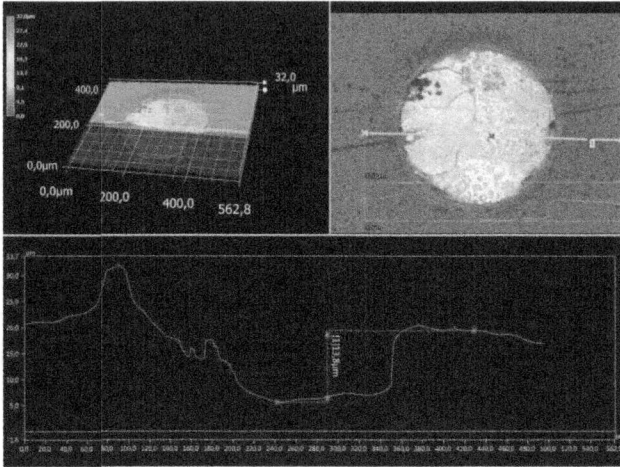

Photo: Height and depth measurements of solder points

3.4 Market Overview

Many countries around the world have a limited number of data recovery companies. If you search the internet you tend to be overwhelmed with the massive number of ads and organic results offered in google. So, what are these other market participants who are trying to get new cases while not actually being a data recovery company? A few of them are computer repair shops and some are true **scammers**.

Many data recovery companies cooperate with computer repair shops that have a limited regional range. These small service providers are **very customer focused** and **deliver a great service** to their customers over decades. Building a **trust relationship** with these shops that really **do a very good job** takes time. They are aware, that they need to protect their reputation as it is what drives clients to them locally.

Computer repair shops can help with small technical issues such as replacing broken drive or reinstalling Windows. They are not able to do a full-scale data recovery as they lack the equipment and amount of incoming jobs to justify the huge investment in equipment and training. Since data recovery companies do not provide IT support, the services of computer repair shops complement perfectly when a client needs his data recovered and his system hardware replaced.

The real problem arises when some computer repair shops **decide to do a complex data recovery job themselves** without following the correct procedures. That is when unpleasant things happen to the drives of their clients. This usually leads to severe data loss for the troubled customer.

3.4.1 Misleading advertising

As previously mentioned, search engines have become inundated with advertising and organic results leading to fake laboratories, who offer data recovery at insane prices or even with quite questionable terms. For consumers it is very difficult to really recognize the difference between the reputable companies and those who are just pure internet marketing agencies.

The more data recovery entrepreneurs have to battle with these internet agencies, the more they have to learn about *search engine optimization, SEM, online advertising, on-page and off-page optimization, backlinks* and so on. You might think, its ok for a DR company to outsource their advertising to an agency.

Unfortunately, there are scammers there too, who try to rip off any kind of small business. I have made my own experience with ads agencies who claimed to use AI for their keyword optimization and were not able to deliver any new business to us – while my own campaigns were generating leads and revenue. As data recovery experts we have had to **educate ourselves on SEO/SEM** in order be visible on page one as the scammers have plenty of resources to flood the search engines. Hence, it is becoming for us all a rat race just to keep up with the scammers who sometimes rip off even our best friends who didn't want to disturb us with their tech problems and got scammed by the black sheep of the data recovery industry. Funnily enough, my own first encounter with the industry was 2 decades ago when my own server drives had a technical issue due to a faulty controller card.

The scammer wanted to charge me a massive amount of money. When I refused, my drives came back with physical damage although they were in perfect condition. At that time, I did not have the knowledge nor the software to recover data from my faulty raid partition. Today, that would not be a big deal for me. Back then that was a horrible shock. Maybe that is what is stuck in my mind when I speak to a person in trouble. I **know how horrible it is to lose data** or to be scammed.

Hence, you will realize that search engines do not place a company on the page because of their good reputation but because they either pay a lot to google ads or make a lot of effort to get their search engine optimization in the race. Some ads are very difficult to differentiate from organic results if you are visiting the search engine pages on a mobile device.

Just keep in mind, there are not a lot of data recovery experts. If they were, we would have 10 football stadiums filled at each conference. Instead, a room for 500 people is big enough to house the experts travelling from places as far as Mexico, **USA**, Panama, UK, Sweden, Colombia, **India**, **Japan** and many other countries to the event in Prague.

3.4.2 Invented laboratory photos

Some market participants take a great affection to creating fake laboratory videos. It is astonishing how the camara can pass through strong walls without getting broken. They even like to create fake set ups of their equipment just to fool the consumer into believing this is all working. If you look closely at the photos of these scam artists, you will notice that these cards are cheap controller cards that wouldn't even function with the drive that is attached to it in the picture.

The manufacturers of the special equipment know where their special tools are in operation as they have country blockers and are tied to the individual data recovery company. If you want to sell part of your equipment, you need to get permission before selling the equipment to another company, even if it is a subsidiary or JV partner.

If you have ever visited their HQs in Russia, you might have had the pleasure to see a **global map with pins in all the locations** where a true <u>data recovery company is operating with their equipment</u>. Just look at the location of the scammer and you will **most likely <u>not find</u> <u>a pin</u>** stuck in that location.

I have even encountered scammers taking cleanroom photos from a high-tech company website and claiming this picture is from their own data recovery lab. The mere fact that the <u>equipment on the photo is not adequate for a data recovery job</u> will not be noticed by most consumers. Some of my colleges in other countries have told me quite some other astonishing stories how they noticed people being misled by websites and advertising.

3.4.3 Black sheep in the data recovery industry

As mentioned already, there is a lot of scamming happening in the industry. Many google results lead to unreal laboratories. Some of them even claim to have no staff in the country they are claiming to be based in. So where is the person who is taking your money? Well, you need to research much deeper. Wait? You are in a hurry and need your data back. You have no time to scan the web to filter out the many traps. Unfortunately google is not really helping you reduce the risk.

So how can you spot the red flags that tell you to keep away for too good to be true offers? Most people who have suffered a data loss will not usually give you testimonials. They will give you referrals by telling friends how good you helped them. Very few really bother to even sign a written testimonial. Taking this fact into consideration, just look at the scammers who operate their websites with lots of video testimonials.

Over the many years being in business, it is difficult to get entrepreneurs or company directors to admit on video that they were not prepared to avoid the need to engage a data recovery expert. So why are these people really giving a testimonial on video that millions of people see all the time? In Europe people are very protective of their privacy and being openly about their short comings is not something people enjoy a lot. So, take these many video testimonials with caution.

For those who argument, video testimonials are ok in other industries: Yes, I have also video testimonials from clients in other industries but data recovery is not an area people will openly come out with having violated ground rules of business. They would put ideas in the tax office people to investigate if the accounting rally matches the stated numbers. Of course, that is a different story.

One of the astonishing ways of some scammers I by using terms of business and contracts that place a fine (EUR 1000) upon the client should their share the offer document with a third party or even talk to other people about this case. This kind of contract fine is illegal in the jurisdiction where they are attempting to keep people from spreading the news about this scammer.

Sometimes even <u>data recovery companies</u> become the <u>victim of scammers</u>. I once had the case where a customer didn't pay us while reselling the service to an unsuspecting client of his. This went as far as to eventually becoming a criminal case as the state prosecutor had to be notified of this unpaid invoice that gradually evolved to a full-scale **list of criminal offences** the scammer had been performing. The police investigator was soon able to put a real name to the suspect based on our description and the **surveillance video of the bank** where he got his fake cheque stamped.

The story went on for a good year as the **suspect was fugitive** as he was wanted for many other known crimes. Eventually a **coincidence** happened that <u>led me to the whereabouts of this person</u>. The police **managed to arrest him** and in court he admitted to the many things he had done, after my testimony and the evidence we had collected in the process of the investigation. We got our money and that was for us then another experience to learn from. As you have noticed there is so much crazy stuff going on that even seasoned data recovery experts need time to spot the red flags.

3.4.4 Can one trust a customer review (page)?

People are questioning review sites and trust sites. They are not to be trusted. That is the reality. It is very easy to fake lots of positive testimonials. If you are strategic about it, you can easily spread in between a few negative comments to make it even look more genuine.

It is the same problem if you want to buy electronics or clothing on the many small and big online stores. You can buy thousands of reviews just for a mere $29. Yes, I get lots of emails every year offering me such "great" services. So why bother providing a great data recovery service, when you can clean your online reputation for just $29 to get lots of positive reviews.

3.4.5 Advertising with extremely low prices

Another nice trap is using extremely low pricing on a website. It is a nice way to get you in the door and then tell you that your case is a very unusually expensive case. Then the data recovery stated as just costing €300 will suddenly cost 4 times the price. That eventually leads to you **paying by far more** that the most diligent data recovery expert will ever charge you. The true data recovery lab will state you a range when you call them as parts cost differently depending on model and source.

In some countries you are required to state the cost in offers and on the website with the sales tax included. The nice trickery used here, is to state the cost excluding sales tax. That is a violation of the law but as long as the consumer does not run to the police, the scammer will **keep you from looking elsewhere** while he increases his profits 20X what would have been reasonable. If you live in the US then that is totally normal and legal to do, but in Europe (and other countries far away) this is not allowed as it is a misleading misrepresentation of facts. As a lab owner in the US reported to our community, he even noticed that scammers were tearing off parts from the drive PCB in order to escalate the costs when the client decided to go to a professional laboratory.

Just keep in mind that there are also labs operating in very poor condition who do not take care. They ignore the industry standards regarding worker health safety and use very bad soldering equipment. As my company is also a supplier for police labs and have been selling a variety of equipment, we have even sold to some of the DR equipment manufacturers special air filters to protect researchers from the health risks of soldering with led that is not led-free.

Data recovery companies are in no way exempt from the standard legal rules on work safety and compliance. So be careful when you see some strange photos on websites.

3.4.6 Global list of data recovery firms

Following list of data recovery firms are based on personal experience with those who attend trainings, conferences and exchange insights with other data recovery professionals.

Photo: Acelabs RAID training in Prague (2016)

I know many of the following data recovery owners as I have met them on several occasions. You either share desks in trainings or at industry conferences. The true DR community helps each other with advice, parts or joint work on new solutions (research).

Country	City	Company	Expert/Owner
Austria	Linz	Kompass Datenrettung	Bela Stirbu
Brazil	São Paulo	Bot Recuperação de Dados	Paulo Braga
	Porto Alegre	InfoDataHD	Raphael Santos
Denmark	Herlufmagle	Quattro Data Recovery	Jens H.S. Tingleff
France	Pantin	Data Up	Nicolas Plée
Germany	Munich	ACATO GmbH	Christian Bartsch
	Berlin	030 Datenrettung Berlin GmbH	Martin Schauerhammer
	Bielefeld	CBL GmbH	
Greece	Athens	DataRecall	George Soulis
		TicTac Data recovery	Panagiotis Pierros & Mike Mingos
Italy	Milan	DataStor	Francesco d' Angelo

	Cagliari, Sardinia	Data Recovery Italia	Claudio Asoni
	Mendoza	Recupero Datos	Adrian Francisconi
Norway	Bergen	RecoverIT AS	Espen Dysvik-Brandt
Portugal	Porto	Bot Recuperação	Thiago Vieira
	Lisbon	HD Rescue	Tiago Colaco
United Kingdom	Sheffield	TRC Ltd.	Chris Sampson
	Peterborough	PC Image Data Recovery Ltd.	Sean Kerrigan
	Cardiff	NANDOFF Data Recovery	Mark Greenwood Jnr
USA	Bala Cynwyd, Pennsylvania	Tri Star Data Revocery	Don Anderson
Serbia	Belgrade	Data Solutions	Nikola Radenkovic
Sweden	Linhamn	PlexData	Daniel Milino

3.4.7 Training and Knowledge Exchange

It is important for data recovery experts to keep updating their knowledge. This is why in non-pandemic times the experts assemble from all continents at the events organized by **Acelabs** and other core manufacturers of specialized equipment. On other occasions we exchange knowledge via zoom, skype or even in closed Facebook groups.

Photo: Presentation on Data recovery for virtual systems during Acelabs Conference in Prague

4 Technical Equipment

This chapter highlights some of today's equipment. Many labs still use a lot of older equipment. As these are gradually being retired, I have not included them in this international edition as you can hardly get hold of them.

4.1 Tools for Hard drive Data recovery

4.1.1 Atola Bandura

This hard drive imaging system can diagnose a drive and copy it. Where the damage is severe you will have to switch to using PC3000.

4.1.2 Acelabs PC3000 Portable/Express

The PC3000 System is available as a portable or built-in computer card.

4.1.3 Acelabs Data Extractor

Besides purchasing the PC3000 Hardware you will need to get a license of their Data Extractor tool:

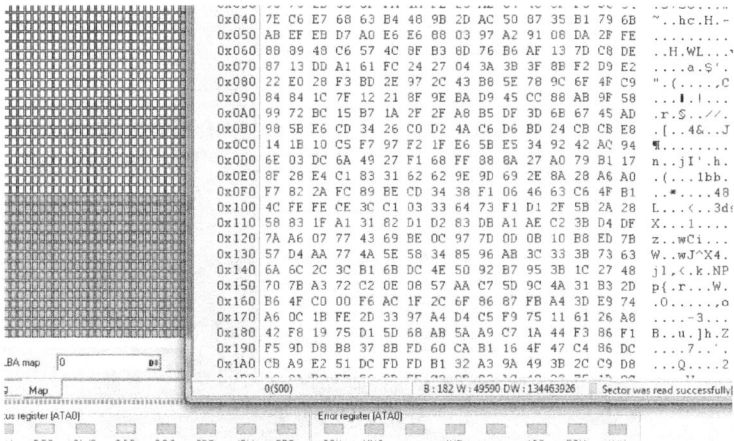

4.1.4 Laminar flow Desktops (cleanrooms)

Opening a drive without a clean room environment can lead to severe data loss. The dust and other pollutants in the air have an adverse effect of the drive's heads as they hover over the rotating disks. The labs I have mentioned in the data recovery list, have such professional equipment and do not have the necessity to publish fake videos like some scammers tend to do in the internet.

This kind of laminar flow desks cost around $5000 - $12000 depending on their country of origin and addons. There are some very poor-quality devices made in China for maybe $2000.

4.1.5 SCSI / SAS Raid Controller

In order to recover data from SCSI or SAS drives you need a different set up than for traditional SATA hard drives. The following picture shows you a SCSI Controller being used with PC3000 SAS:

Here is an example using a special adapter card:

4.2 Equipment for Data recovery from memory cards and USB pen drives

4.2.1 PC3000 Flash

Starting to use PC3000 Flash is by far easier. In the last 10 years their technology has massively improved. They even came up with some very ingenious solutions to reduce the amount of necessary soldering. This awakens great memories of being training at their HQ in Rostov on Don (Russia). Now you can even attend these courses in Prague.

4.2.2 VNR – Visual NAND Reconstructor (Rusolut)

With the VNR system you can extract data from chips extracted out of a variety of devices (USB-Sticks, Memory cards, smartphones). For more details jump to the VNR segment on smartphone data recovery.

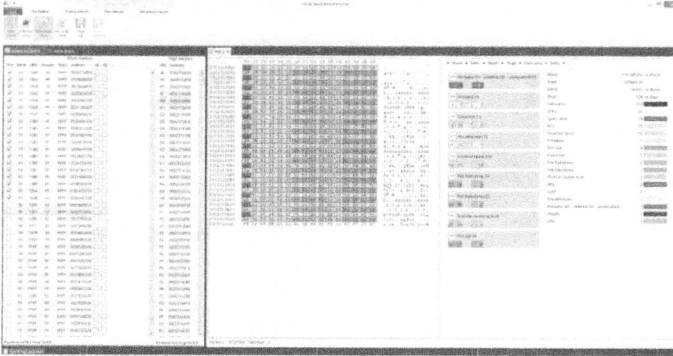

Since the trainings provide quite a lot of information, I eventually created my own training manual to help me refresh my knowledge if I am not working on a particular type of case from a few months. When I look at the 200-page manual I notice this is just the peak of the iceberg. The document keeps growing as VNR is further developed.

4.2.3 Soldering Tool for PCBs and memory chips

This bracket helps you hold the PCB or chip in position while you are soldering.

4.2.4 Rework stations

In order to unsolder chips with higher memory density you need to use professional rework stations. Otherwise, the risk of killing the chip is extremely high.

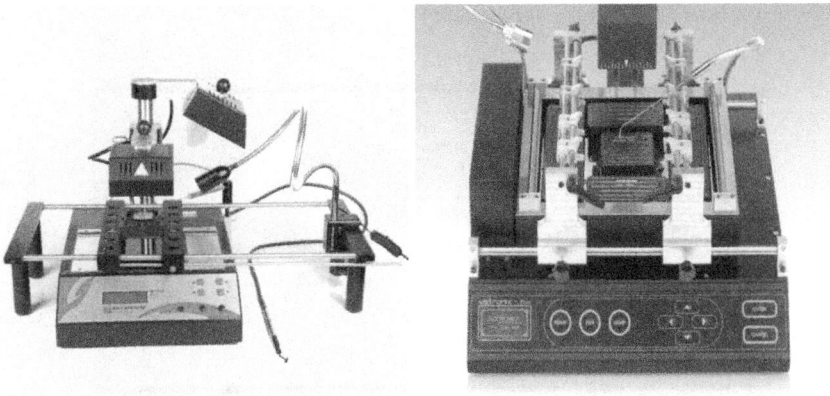

4.2.5 Stencils for reballing chips

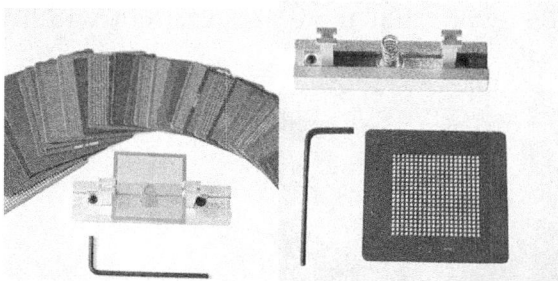

4.2.6 Holder for reballing

4.2.7 Special smartphone reballing kits

You will need to use stencils to reball a chip in a rework station.

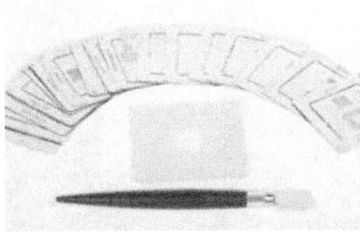

4.2.8 Solder Wick

In order to help clean the contacts of chips you use solder wick. It attracts the solder to the copper wick. Thereby you can softly remove the solder and ensure there is no residue left on each pin. Dirty pins on a chip can lead to a short circuit or malefaction during the reading of the chip. Be aware that there are different width and types of quality.

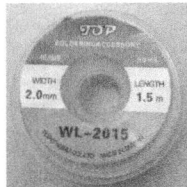

4.2.9 Solder Station

You will need a solder station with the right kind of solder pins.

4.2.10 Sucking pens and other helpful gadgets

In order to remove the chip from the PCB after it has been unsoldered, it is recommended to use a sucking pen. You can also use tweezers.

4.3 Equipment for smartphone data recovery

4.3.1 VNR (Rusolut)

This is what the Visual Nand Reconstructor looks like. This powerful solution was developed by the Russian company Rusolut.

As the technology was being improved the amount of recoverable data has increased.

| DATA | SA | BCH oder ECC Code |

Photo: Examples extracted from my presentation at
German Central Police (2015 / BKA)

As you can see their tool is quite complex. It is highly advisable to
attend their onsite trainings in Warsaw.

Photo: VNR Reader and Chip Socket adapter

Together with *Sasha Sheremetov* (CTO of Rusolut) I have had the
pleasure to test different methodologies for recovering data from
smartphones. At that time our arsenal of reference devices was quite
large (ca. 2000 cell phones / 5000 Smartphones) and allowed Rusolut
to try out phones which they had not had access to before.

Photo: Training in Poland with Rusolut in 2015
(I am sitting on the left)

4.3.2 NuProg

Using Nuprog helps you read UFS Chips. It supports UFS and eMMC/eMCP chips built in newer Smartphones.

4.3.3 Easy JTag Devices

With "easy Jtag" you can **read the chip memory of active Smartphones** while they are **switched on**. This is not possible with some brands anymore as the **newer phones** have other types of connectors that <u>make it impractical to use jtagging</u> in order to read the memory.

4.3.4 LCD-Separators

You need to use an LCD-Separator to remove the display of the smartphone as many of them are stuck to the frame. If you can't get the display off then you might have encountered a repaired phone that was stuck with a heat resistant M3 glue.

4.4 Software Products for Data Recovery

There are many tools that can help you recover data. The professional tools cost a substantial amount of money. You might also need to take the time to learn how to properly handle these tools.

4.4.1 UFS Explorer

You can use UFS Raid Explorer to recover data from complex Raid Systems. This is not a tool designed for consumers but for true experts.

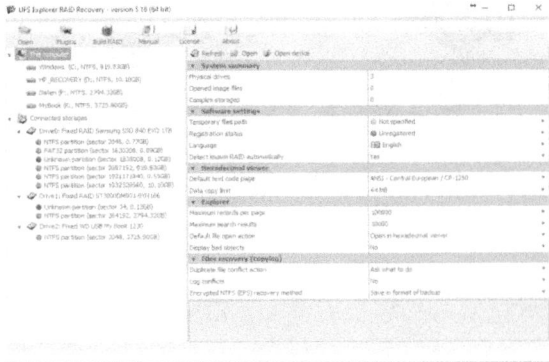

4.4.2 JPEG Repair Kit

As previously mentioned, user do tend to damage their pictures by trying wrong data recovery methods. Our Dutch colleague Joep van Steen (Disktuna.com) developed his own software "JPG Repair kit" to address these unfortunately situations:

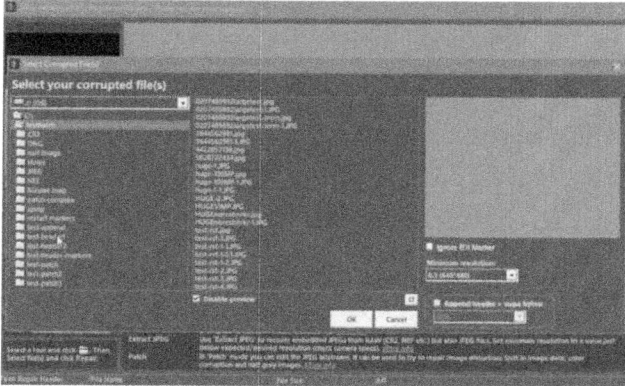

Joep is also working on a tool to repair videos. I have bought video repair tools from Indian companies but like many other colleagues, we never found the tools could cope with the damaged video material.

5 Data Security in Companies

Large organisations need to improve their data security. In previous decades this was done by using tape drives and highly expensive equipment. As the size of data sky rockets the challenge is to get it stored outside of the organisation where no hacker and no ransomware can get hold of the backup.

5.1 Wrong security approaches

some business leaders totally underestimate the risk of experiencing a data loss. They think their backup will always do a great job to help them out of a disaster. Unfortunately, this often does not work properly. Hence, the best approach is to work on a disaster recovery plan.

Some equipment is massively neglected and left to decay. Even if there is well training IT staff on premises, they can't keep the equipment properly maintained if their superiors and hindering them from devoting the necessary time and effort.

5.1.1 How a NAS becomes a black hole for its data

Using a Network Area Storage System is supposed to help businesses handle the ever-growing amount of data to store. The complexity of these systems is causing problems in small and large organisations. Wrong settings and incorrect response to a drive failure corrupts the data. If there is too much fiddle around then the data is permanently useless.

5.1.2 Errors in IT Consulting

Some IT consulting companies like to promote equipment that is not of benefit to their client. This eventually leads to data loss or recuring system failures. If the equipment is known to be incompatible for the intended use, then this even increases the risk for a business client who is relying on the advice of this particular multinational IT consultancy. Unfortunately, some consultancies prefer to cover up their wrong advice by getting rid of the experts who highlight this dangerous misconfiguration (Eccles, Krzus, 2010).

5.1.3 Using Cobit to increase security

It is a good idea to use Cobit (*Control Objectives for Information and Related Technology*) to make sure your information technology is well secured. Some department leaders do not want to take the necessary precautions until their employer suffers a terrible loss.

Photo: bottom side of an EMMC memory chip

It is a true responsibility of management to make sure their IT security matches the to be expected risks (Asma, 2011). American auditors follow the SOX rules to make sure the requirements have been met (Braiotta, 2010).

Once an organisation has recognized the need to improve security and awareness their risk of losing data and their competitive advantage is dropping substantially.

6 How to prevent data loss

In order to avoid losing data, you need to take precautions ahead of time. It is a smart idea to take the advice from data recovery experts and data centre consultants if you are running a large business. Even some small hints from a DR expert can save you a lot of pain in the future. There are some basic steps to mitigate your risk exposure.

6.1 Having an overview of your infrastructure

The better your infrastructure has been documented the better your ability to respond to unusual situations. You need to know which systems are installed in your data centre and in your office space. People often forget the odd NAS station beneath the desk of the head of marketing. You can make your work a little easier by using IT inventory tools that scan the network for devices. When you install the agents of this system on the different devices it will even keep up to date the information about what is installed and the current versions. If there is some security alert regarding to particular software releases you can quickly spot the weak points in your network and update them before any hacker or virus can infiltrate your company network.

Now keep this in mind: small components that fail might lead to a chain reaction. This would potentially put your entire network out of order. Evaluate the risks each component might present to your network and see how you can mitigate the risks. Sometimes a small power surge protection would be better than nothing. Also note when generating the equipment list you is responsible for managing and using that system. There can be 2 totally different parties involved with that particular device. Also rate the risk they are potentially exposing the network using a number range from 1 - 10.

6.2 Evaluation of potential Weaknesses

6.2.1 Analyse the strategic zones

You need to evaluate the strategic importance of systems in your network. If your mainframe fails and your factories stop producing products then you have visualized a potential threat, consequence and the source of the risk. Another typical risk zone is your email server. If that gets infected it could infect lots of office computers and even spread across countries into your subsidiaries. This could freeze your entire organisation.

Create a catalogue that lists all the areas of risk, the impact they can have on the organisation and how you intend to reduce the risk exposure. In some jurisdictions auditors are required to do IT audits to confirm there are no severe risks that could damage the company's financial situation that it would hurt the investors or shareholders.

6.2.2 Analyse your current state

How about getting an overview of your current infrastructure and identifying is current state? You need to know where you are at this time. Decide on what your ideal situation would be and work from there to fill the gaps between the current state and your optimum state. You can even use a benchmark to get an idea what is an acceptable level in your particular industry.

6.3 To Do List

6.3.1 Creating your action list

Once you know your risk exposure and the SWAT like analysis has given you a map of problematic areas in your company you need to take action. Make a list of the actions you will have to perform in a timely manner in order to fix the issues or at least mitigate the risk exposure to an acceptable level.

6.3.2 Plan for a crisis

You need to be prepared for the eventuality of a crisis knocking at your door. Recently a data centre of a large cloud provider suffered a severe outage because a fire broke out inside the facility. Some clients had not taken precautions and just relied on the provider to have a backup of their data although they themselves had not permitted backups. Nevertheless, this situation is a very unpleasant event for the provider and the business clients affected by the fire.

An additional helpful precaution is to create workflow maps. This makes it easier to identify bottle necks and develop checklists and response plan that fit to the situation properly.

6.3.3 Publication of crisis response strategies

It is important to not only have a crisis emergency plan but also to let people know about it. They have to be able to find the document in time and be told exactly what to do in an emergency. A good approach is also to add a serial number to that document and a date so that people can recognize when their copy of the document is outdated!

6.3.4 Handling internal conflicts

In large organisations people tend to desire climbing the ranks at the expense of the organisation. They are willing to expose the company to sever risks in order to blame management.

6.3.5 Introduction of a Helpdesk System

Every large organisation needs to have a central point of contact so that user can report technical issues. A small problem might escalate to a substantial problem. Similar situations like system failures that appear due to melting network cabling or other problems can be quickly identified as a massive issue if users address their help requests to a helpdesk. Creating an uncontrollable chaos by calling different people in the IT department just clogs up an organisation and limits its ability to respond properly.

7 Protection

In order to ensure a security concept is going to be adequate for the business, you need to regularly check that the control systems are in operation and people have understood how to apply them (Braiotta et al., 2010).

7.1 Degree of Implementation

Organisations generally need to pay more attention to how critical data is stored. I have seen large companies store employee records on USB drives. This kind of data should actually be well protected inside a SaaS application and not in a device that can easily be removed.

When you are trying to assess the degree of implementation then you need to set specific criteria. Thereby, you can compare your desired situation with the situation your audits are showing.

As you scan the range of equipment and software used by a company, you will need to select the required audit team members so that they have the knowledge and skills to perform an IT audit properly (Braiotta et al., 2010, p. 217).

7.1.1 How regulators affect us (SEC, NYSE)

The New Yorker Exchange has set rules that require the company leadership to pay proper attention at managing risks. This has led to the introduction of risk management strategies as there corporates are trying to create rules and standards to comply (NYSE Rule 303A.07©(iii)(D)).

Companies without sufficient internal expertise or human capacity are required to source it from outside their organisation. This has led to British companies adapting the "**Combined Code**" (2006, par.C.2.) as a way to ensure their shareholders are protected.

As you will have noticed this topic can take up a full book and it would definitely require much more space to provide helpful checklists and best practice examples. Hence, as topic is growing in complexity, I have decided to provide more information on my website so you can easily download it and use it in your business.

7.2 Device destruction

You need to have a backup plan when your company has to dispose of all the old devices. In 2017 we had to get a massive amount of obsolete donor drives professionally shredded by a specialized company.

Photo: a full-size data security bin with lots of drives to be destroyed for us by Reisswolf

8 Final Thoughts

Is there something you can take away after reading all these technology and market insights? The core reason for loosing data is usually the user or material fatigue. Avoid trying to recover your data on your own as you are most likely going to increase the damage. This might even lead to your 2nd option of getting help from a professional data recovery firm becoming pointless. Saving some money is not worth the aggravation and consequent data loss.

Nevertheless, you need to be aware that there are some scammers out there waiting to rip you off. They have no data recovery equipment and no expertise other than creating multiple websites offering you a great promise. They even make the effort to create fake testimonial videos.

You will have seen the list of professional data recovery experts and their companies. I have had the pleasure of the last 15+ years to get to know many of them. Their expertise is a great asset for our community and our clients.

9 Autor's Profile

You can find out more about the author and what his current focus is on by visiting his website at **meetchrisbartsch.com**

Christian started to program computers in 1996 and eventually looked deeper into the hardware side of his equipment. He holds a multitude of certifications (MCT, MCSE+I, IT Project, IT forensics, CFE, etc.). He also worked for some of the top brands (**BMW**, Siemens/OSRAM, **KPMG**) and now ACATO.

9.1 Speeches

Christian has been providing insights into a selected area of expertise in his speeches (starting in 2002). These included presentations for the German central police (2015 BKA), for the house of commerce and its IT security days (on recommendation of BSI 2015/2017), and many others. This also included a presentation at the University of Applied science in Aachen (2016).

Photo: Me presenting at the house of commerce in Darmstadt during the BSI Security Event (IHK Darmstadt, 2017)

9.2 Radio, TV and Magazine Articles

Christian has appeared multiple times (2012/2013) in the popular science program "**Galileo**" which is broadcasted nationwide on **Pro7**. Even radio interviews on **BR2**, **Deutsche Welle** and other channels were part of the adventure. Not to mention the appearance on the news channel **n-tv** (Feb. 2016) providing insights into smartphone forensics and data recovery.

Photo: Me being interviewed for the popular German science program "Galileo" (to be broadcasted on Pro7)

This was a great opportunity to provide journalists a backstage insight into how data recovery companies work and how much equipment they tend to need for the wide range of cases.

Photo: Filming in my lab for the news broadcaster n-tv

Photo: Interview in the Digital Photo Magazine

9.2.1 Vision for the future

During a conversation with *Apple co-founder* **Steve Wozniak** his ideas around training and continued education were confirmed by Steve.

Photo: Interview with Steve Wozniak (Nov. 2017)

If you take the time to listen to the podcast of the author which is available on Spotify and audible you will recognize there is a lot coming towards us in regards to business, hardware and IT security.

10 Bibliography

Following literature assisted me in writing this book and therefore I am adding them here as references:

Asma, J. (2011), "Von Modellen und Risiken", KPMG AG WPG, in: „Kes – Die Zeitschrift für Informationssicherheit", March 2011 edition, SecuMedia Verlags-GmbH, p. 6-8

Braiotta, Jr. L., Gazzaway, R.T., Colson, R., Ramamoorti, S. (2010), "The Audit Committee Handbook", 5th Edition, New Jersey, Wiley, ISBN 078-0-470-60822-7, pp. 215-240

Brucnail, J.M. (2011), "Solid state deterioration", published 26.06.2011, accessed on 08.12.2012, http://www.techradar.com/news/computing-components/storage/how-ssds-work-969473/2#articleContent

Cannon, D. (2011), "CISA - Certified Information Systems Auditor - Study Guide ", 3rd Edition, Indianapolis, Wiley, ISBN 978-0-470-61010-7

Eccles, R.G, Krzus, M.P. (2010), "One Report – Integrated Reporting for a Sustainable Strategy", New Jersey, Wiley, ISBN 978-0-470-58751-5, p.117

Glenn, W., Lowe, S., Maher, J. (2007), "Microsoft Exchange Server 2007 – Das Handbuch", Unterschleißheim, Microsoft Press Deutschland, ISBN 978-3-86645-116-2, pp. 73, 381, 645

Navarro J., Karlins M. (2012), „Menschen lesen", 8. Edition, mvg Verlag, ISBN978-3-86882-213-7

Olson P. (2012), "Inside Anonymous ", Redline Verlag, ISBN 978-3-86881-349-4

Shook, J., Maher, H., O'Neil, W.T. (2011), "The Lawyer's Guide to eDiscovery Technology for Dummies", Hoboken, Wiley, ISBN 978-1-118-07338-4, pp. 3-22

Shook, J., Maher, H., O'Neil, W.T. (2011), "The Technologist's Guide to eDiscovery Technology for Dummies", Hoboken, Wiley, ISBN 978-1-118-07338-4, p. 3

Toshiba (2012), "Solid State Drive", accessed on 08.12.2012, http://storage.toshiba.eu

Wikipedia (2012), "COBIT", accessed on 18.08.2012, http://de.wikipedia.org/wiki/COBIT

Wikipedia (2011), "USB flash drive", accessed on 08.12.2012, http://en.wikipedia.org/wiki/USB_flash_drive

Wikipedia (2012), "Hard disk drive", accessed on 09.12.2012, http://en.wikipedia.org/wiki/Hard_disk_drive

Wikipedia (2012), "Backplane", last adaptation 28.07.2012, accessed on 09.12.2012, http://de.wikipedia.org/wiki/Backplane

Made in the USA
Las Vegas, NV
29 May 2025